Let's make more smiles!
Encouraging Positive Behaviour

All children exhibit challenging behaviours from time to time, but when the behaviour becomes dangerous or harmful we need to intervene and decide how and when we should do this.

This book has been written to support those working or living with children who display challenging behaviour. Author Wendy Usher uses over 30 years of experience both as a parent of a disabled young woman and as a professional bringing insights and ideas in an easy to understand and practical way.

The various case studies and stories are true; however names and details have been changed to protect the identities of the children and families concerned.

This book is one of a series published by The Play Doctors supporting inclusion. Each book provides thoughts and resources to help adults work with all children to ensure they are offered the same chances and experiences as others.

All rights reserved. No part of this publication may be reproduced or transmitted in any form or by any means, electronically or mechanically, including photocopying, recording or any information storage or retrieval system, without prior permission in writing from the publisher The Play Doctors Ltd.

All photographs in this book are accredited to iStockphoto.com or produced with written permission of the parents and/or guardians of the children discussed and of the children themselves. The names of both adults and the children have been changed to protect their privacy.

Second Edition 2012
Published by The Play Doctors Ltd
first published 2011
© Wendy Usher
ISBN Number: 978-0-9566690-4-9

Content

	Page No
Content	
Chapter One Setting the scene, an introduction	1
Chapter Two Exploring challenging behaviour	14
Chapter Three Looking behind the behaviour	23
Chapter Four Setting the boundaries	44
Chapter Five Consequences of behaviour	61
Chapter Six Encouraging Positive Behaviour	67
Chapter Seven Summary and Further Information	83

This book is dedicated with thanks to my family!
Wendy Usher

Chapter One:
Setting the scene: an introduction

We can all get discouraged at times when we watch our children display a range of behaviour that we feel is unacceptable. Some behaviour may cause embarrassment and be socially unacceptable. Other behaviour may be dangerous, causing damage to self, others or property.

Certain behaviours need to be dealt with straightaway, particularly if dangerous. Some types of behaviour need longer-term assessment and observation to understand what is behind the action, so that we can know how to best manage it.

Behaviour itself is a form of communication. It expresses emotions in verbal and non-verbal ways. Sometimes, it is difficult to 'read' the messages behind the behaviour when we are just focusing on the actions taking place.

There are immediate steps that need to be put into place to ensure safety. There are also times where we need to be patient, observe, listen and consider what the issues are behind the behaviour.

If behaviour is a form of communication, what is the communication behind the behaviour?

Let's start at the beginning by exploring our own behaviour traits. Begin by imagining you are presenting a very important report to a large group of people. On the day of the presentation you may be nervous and slightly apprehensive. This means that you are trying hard to concentrate on what you are going to say, and you do not want to speak to others, be distracted or disturbed. You may be 'short' with others who speak to you and break your concentration.

© The Play Doctors Ltd.

Next, you go to your car to drive to work and find you have a flat tyre. On trying to use the spare, you find it also has a puncture. This is making you late and, in addition to your nervousness, you are now getting apprehensive and worried.

Going back into the house, you find that the phone is inexplicably out of order. Your mobile has run out of credit, and you cannot phone for a taxi.

Now you are beginning to feel anger and frustration in addition to anxiety.

We could go on, but the picture is starting to build of how your feelings escalate, your frustration mounts and your behaviour changes. Each of us is an individual and will react differently. What would your reaction be? Perhaps you would kick the tyre (or maybe the cat), swear and punch the wall. Perhaps you would be logical and calm, or want to cry?

Our behaviour is communicating our feelings. But, if someone just saw the behaviour pattern, they would not necessarily know the reason and therefore would be unable to offer help and support.

Exploring potential reasons

Let's start to think of the reasons behind behaviour. Consider what makes you angry. You may have thought of:

Unfairness; unjust action; defence mechanisms (self-defence and defending others); other people's response and behaviour to situations; inability to break down a barrier; or perhaps something that is beyond your control.

Does your behaviour and emotion change based on the environment and how you feel? Do you:

- Get short tempered if you have a headache or are in pain?
- Have less patience when you feel very hot?
- Have less tolerance for others when you need to go somewhere urgently, such as the toilet?
- Feel down and lethargic on cold, wet, dark days?
- Find your feelings are affected by hormones (both male and female)?

© The Play Doctors Ltd.

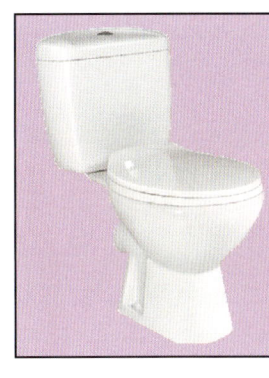

> **Henry gets angry when he needs the toilet. However, he does not necessarily recognise the sensation of having a full bladder, particularly when he is playing or doing something he wants to do.**
>
> **The play workers need to remind Henry to go the toilet on a regular basis. Once he has been, his temper improves.**

Your feelings may reflect those of a child exhibiting unacceptable behaviour. Often, we judge too quickly without knowing what the communication is behind the behaviour. It is difficult to know how to put strategies in place that help the root causes if we do not know what those root causes are.

Generally, very young children misbehave because they have not learnt how to react to feelings and needs in acceptable ways. Toddlers: may have short attention spans; be bored; be curious; imitate others; respond against others' behaviour (self-preservation); want to be independent; may be frustrated, anxious, fearful or just excited.

Even though we may understand the reasons behind the behaviour being exhibited we must not excuse the behaviour being displayed. It is still essential to ensure the child or young person understands if the behaviour is acceptable or not. Agreed boundaries must be put into place, and we need the skills to reinforce positive behaviour appropriately.

This book explores these issues, and more. We use a number of case studies and short stories following a group of children and young people. We identify how they behave, how their behaviour affects others and how adults can help them modify their actions.

The book is not a psychology tool or a manual on behaviour management. Instead, it offers an insight into ways of supporting and improving behaviour using experience gained over thirty years. It considers the issues from both the adult's and the child's perspective. There are many suggestions and strategies provided. The book is designed to help you think 'outside the box' and relate ideas to your own particular situation.

We explore what works well, and why, and what has not worked so well. Remember, what works well for a time may need refreshing at a later date. We also explore our own behaviour as adults and assess how this affects the children we work or live with.

We recognise that it is not easy, and dealing with poor behaviour is very stressful. This in itself affects our own behaviour; we also need support and understanding.

Throughout this book we follow four children and young people who display a range of challenging behaviour. The case studies and stories look at different times in their lives and describe various aspects of their personal stories. Additional short stories about other children or young people are also used.

Henry is 8 years old; he lives at home with his parents and his younger sister, Georgia. He was diagnosed with Attention Deficit Hyperactivity Disorder (ADHD) when he was 5. He attends his local school and has a Teaching Support Assistant who works with him two days per week.

Henry enjoys sport and physical activity. He has a particular interest in football. He and his father support Manchester United.

During the school day Henry finds it very difficult to sit still and continually disrupts lessons, getting angry if he does not get his own way. He attends an after school club, where he often displays anger at other children and adults, occasionally culminating in violence. Henry uses swear words regularly, and the after school club has received complaints from other parents and are on the verge of excluding him.

Jack is 14 years old; he lives with his grandparents, who have bought him up since he was 8, after his dad was sent to prison.

He enjoys being with his mates, drinking and music. He attends the local school, although he 'bunks off' regularly. However, when he does attend, he is very good at art.

Jack displays challenging behaviour. He will not comply when asked, answers back, swears and will get violent on occasion. He has been in trouble with the police for hitting his grandmother, although she did not want to press charges. He is not interested in school work and mucks around in class when he attends. He is known to bully younger students and is part of a gang of young people who 'hang around' on the streets and have been accused of antisocial behaviour.

© The Play Doctors Ltd.

Leanne is 6 years old; she lives with her parents, three brothers and two sisters. She attends her local school with two other siblings.

She enjoys dancing and singing and being the centre of attention. Leanne likes using her voice, shouting above others and answering back. If she feels that others are receiving more attention than her she will push in and take over.

Leanne tries her hardest to please, but in fact alienates staff by not complying with requests.

She gets distracted trying to 'help' and tell others what to do. She has few friends; most children try to avoid her, and those she calls friends are bossed around by her.

Leanne has a response to everything and will argue constantly. She can be violent and has tried to push her mum down the stairs. She has trashed her own bedroom, stolen sweets, lies and cheats, and has temper tantrums. Her parents are very concerned and wonder if it is a phase she is going through or whether she has a behavioural disorder.

Sharmain is 15 years old; she currently lives with foster parents and has been in care since she was 12. She attends the local school but does not make friends easily. She keeps herself to herself and does not respond well to adults.

Sharmain tends to ignore you if you are speaking to her; she will turn away, shrug her shoulders, roll her eyes or shake her head, and sometimes just walk off. She does not say much, verbalising in grunts and tuts.

Her teacher and foster mum are worried because they think she may be self harming but they have not seen any physical evidence of this. They also think she may be stealing.

She attends the local youth group and sits isolated in the corner, watching what goes on but not joining in. Previously, at school, she has shown an interest in working with younger children. She responds well to her 1-year-old foster sister, but on her own terms, not complying with requests from her foster parents.

Every child or young person we are living or working with is an individual with their own personal story. We don't always know what is going on in their lives and certainly do not know what they are thinking.

We respond to behaviour based on our own expectations, judgements and values. These may be affected by our:

- Previous experience and upbringing
- Background, culture and ethnicity
- Educational experience
- Gender and age
- Religion

Various cultures have different levels of acceptance in relation to how children behave. What may seem 'socially challenging' to one culture may be seen as normal to another.

Take, for example, a family who generally communicate by shouting and fighting. The child has been brought up understanding that this is the way to communicate and win an argument.

There have been no negotiation skills taught by the family. Therefore, our expectation of how the child should behave is unrealistic. Until the appropriate behaviour has been taught or role modelled, the child may not know that there are choices to be made in how he responds to others.

Jack's grandfather had been bought up in a violent and highly-disciplined home. When Jack went to live with his grandparents he was told to keep quiet and to keep out of his grandad's way.

If he did something, his grandad felt was wrong, he was hit with a belt or clipped round the ear. His family did not see anything wrong with this as it was how all the children had been bought up, including Jack's dad.

At 10 years old, Jack began to have difficulty at school and after school club. He used violence first before considering negotiation or discussion.

© The Play Doctors Ltd.

Here, we can see how the role model of the grandfather was reflected in the child's behaviour. The culture of violence in the family is unlikely to change so therefore Jack needs to understand what the school and after school club see as appropriate behaviour. This involves giving Jack alternative behaviours rather than dealing with problems through violence.

Some cultures look down on children, particularly girls. They are seen as chattels to be told what to do and are not respected in the same way as males. Others still feel that children should be seen and not heard. This may affect a person's self-confidence and self-esteem.

> **While living at home, from the age of 8 Sharmain was expected to take on the role of doing the household chores: cooking, cleaning and clearing up after her father and brothers. This was the cultural norm.**
>
> **Sharmain lost the ability to play out with her friends or invite friends to play at her house. As soon as she came back from school she was told what to do and did not have the ability to make her own choices.**

The backgrounds of children and young people will influence how they behave. Although we may not always know their history, we still need to deal with the behaviour in the 'here and now'.

We must not forget that some forms of behaviour may be part of a wider picture: that the child may have an underlying condition that may or may not have been diagnosed. Some behaviour can be attributed to particular impairments, such as autism and Attention Deficit Disorders (ADD). We will explore this throughout the book.

> **Henry experiences sensory overload and cannot cope with too many sensory experiences at the same time. When an adult tries to talk to him, Henry will not hold eye contact. The adult assumes, because of his body language, that he is not listening. However, if the question: "What did I just say?" is asked, Henry is able to repeat the sentence or phrase word for word.**

Henry finds it very difficult to both look and listen at the same time. When he holds eye contact and concentrates visually, he sometimes loses part of his audio sense and misses words being said. This particular trait is associated with ADD and needs to be understood by those working with Henry and accepted.

Henry may be able to repeat a request, but still not comply. This behaviour needs to be challenged, but the lack of eye contact is not dangerous. The adult has made an assumption that Henry is not listening without understanding that he listens with little or no eye contact.

> "Henry, listen to me. I know you are not listening. You are not looking at me."
>
> "Henry, I've told you to listen to me. Well what did I say?"

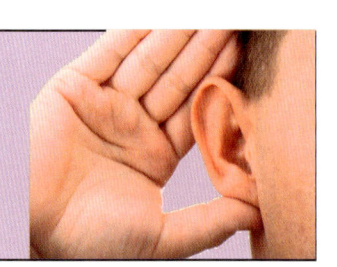

We all have different levels of what we class as acceptable behaviour. It is essential that, when we decide on boundaries and responses, they are consistent between all adults working or living with the child or young person.

We also need to recognise that children will challenge boundaries, and these need to change as children grow. Boundaries need to be agreed by all parties. If the child or young person does not understand why they are expected to behave in a certain way, and do not agree with the rules imposed, they may rebel and disobey, particularly if they feel the rules are unjust.

Hearing the voices of adults

Before starting to write this book, we wanted to ensure it reflected the needs and wishes of adults living or working with children and young people exhibiting challenging behaviour. We asked a range of parents and practitioners what types of behaviour they were dealing with, and what would be useful for them in the form of a book.

All those interviewed agreed that there was no magic wand to be waved and that a range of strategies needed to be put into place. They also agreed that no 'one size fits all'. What works well with one child will not work with the next. Adults asked for ideas and strategies and wanted to know how others had handled similar situations.

This book reflects these thoughts, and provides a range of insights, ideas and strategies. It will to help you think creatively about how you might try to manage a particular challenge.

Parents and workers identified the types of behaviours they felt were challenging. We were able to break them down into two key areas: physical challenges; and emotional challenges. These include actions that are: harmful to self; harmful to others; socially unacceptable; dangerous behaviour; and those actions designed to challenge authority.

We were also told that 'young people's attitude' was an issue. It is difficult to define the word 'attitude'. What does this mean in reality? It needs breaking down and translating into a series of particular behaviours, for instance: head movements; ignoring; raising eyes; shrugging shoulders; talking back; and so on. Most people interviewed defined 'attitude' under the 'emotional' category.

The list on the following page was compiled from the research. It shows the types of behaviour that adults recorded as causing most concern. The list is not exhaustive and we recognised that we are all faced with new challenges every day.

Physical

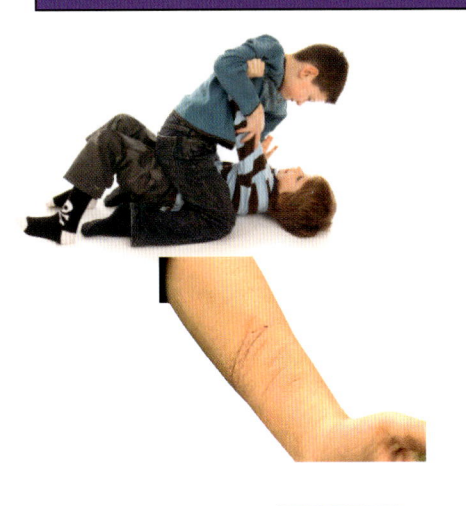

- **Harm to others, including:** aggression; kicking; biting; punching; scratching; pinching; pulling; pushing; throwing; snatching; fighting; sexual overtures (inappropriate touching)

- **Self-harm, including:** cutting; biting; pulling out hair; scratching; eating disorders; drugs; drink; self-induced sleep deprivation

- **Harm to property, including:** vandalism; destroying/harming own and others' property; throwing furniture; kicking walls; breaking windows; graffiti

- **Other behaviour, including:** tantrums; not taking turns; stamping; physical bullying; stealing; running away

© The Play Doctors Ltd.

Emotional

- **Vocal, including:** swearing; answering back; shouting; screaming; grunting; whistling; verbal aggression; emotional drama; bullying; lying and cheating (deception); sexually-based comments; public humiliation; behaviour designed to cause maximum embarrassment

- **Non-vocal, including:** excessive and exaggerated body language; avoiding eye contact; pretending not to hear; crying and dramatics; non-verbal bullying (including cyber bullying)

- **Other behaviour, including:** deliberately breaking rules/boundaries; manipulation; playing adults against each other

Other behaviour that caused concern included:

- **Inattention/hyperactivity, including:** a lack of concentration; flitting and fidgeting; constant movement and noise making; inability to pay attention

- **Stereotypical behaviour, including:** temper tantrums; repetitive behaviours such as rocking, flapping, circling and echolalia (repeating words, phrases or behaviour of others)

The last two types of behaviour are often associated with impairments such as autism and ADHD, and can be difficult to stop. Children on the autism spectrum may have difficulty in communicating, being in social situations and understanding what is going to happen next (lack of imagination). Some behaviour traits that children display act as self-distraction activities. Here, the child concentrates on the behaviour, rather than whatever is causing them anxiety. An example may be a child on the autism spectrum spinning in a circle, holding their hands over their ears. This cuts down on outside noise and other sensory overload.

© The Play Doctors Ltd.

We have all seen a child in a supermarket throwing a tantrum because they cannot get what they want. They use the behaviour as a means to an end. The behaviour becomes embarrassing for the parent/guardian and it is easier to give in. The child gets what they want and the behaviour has been reinforced. When they want the same thing again, they will behave in the same way.

The management of behaviour is a joint responsibility between both adult and child/young person. How we respond will affect how the child responds. We may find ourselves excusing behaviour because the child has had a poor history or underlying condition. This will not do the child or young person any favours in the future. We all have to learn how to act appropriately and behave responsibly.

To ensure that there is balance in this book, we also wanted to listen to the voices of children and young people. We asked a group aged between 5 and 16 whether they felt they ever exhibited any challenging behaviour. We had surprisingly honest responses. Young people themselves recognised that some of their own behaviour was not acceptable, and knew that they needed to have rules and boundaries put into place.

When asked what kind of behaviour they thought was unacceptable the responses were similar to those of the adults. However, they also felt that the behaviour of the adults influenced their own behaviour.

> **"If she didn't shout at me, I wouldn't shout at her."** (5-year-old boy speaking about his mum)
>
> **"The play workers do not obey the rules. Why are there different rules for the staff and us?"** (9-year-old girl speaking about an after school club)
>
> **"She does not want to be here, you can tell. She does not like us so we do not like her."** (13-year-old boy speaking about his teacher)
>
> **"It's fun to see her being scared. I'm smaller than her but she is frightened of me."** (15-year-old girl speaking about a foster parent)
>
> **"He swears, so I do too."** (6-year-old boy speaking about a parent)

© The Play Doctors Ltd.

When asked why they carried on behaving in the way they did, these were some of their responses:

> "I get told off but that's about all. Nothing happens so I do it again."
> "If I behave badly I get sent to the quiet room. I like it there."
> "I like behaving badly so when I do something good I get a star for the chart. If I am good all the time, I don't get any stars."
> "When I break things I get into trouble but I get bought new things so it's worth it."
> "I get really angry and I need to take it out on someone. I don't always mean to take it out on Mum but she's there."
> "I steal things to impress my mates."
> "I don't know why I behave like I do. I know it's wrong but I can't help myself."

The last bullet point indicates that not everyone knows why they do what they do. The behaviour displayed is a result of emotion. Emotions are difficult to define, especially for an individual who may have a social communication impairment. Many young people recognise their own behaviour. They are unhappy at the way they behave, but find themselves unable to stop, and feel 'out of control'.

Many behaviour management strategies look at helping children and young people identify emotions, providing alternative routes to express these emotions rather than by exhibiting challenging behaviour.

Jessica has Aspergers Syndrome. At school she has to abide by the rules. She finds it difficult to cope with so much sensory stimulation and gets very tired when she is concentrating so hard.

On returning home from school, Jessica feels angry and frustrated. She needs a mechanism to release her pent-up emotions and frustration. Her choice of behaviour is to physically release her aggression in the form of scratching and biting her younger sister.

This results in retaliation, and a negative cycle continues between the siblings. Mum gets involved and the family end up arguing.

© The Play Doctors Ltd.

We recognise that Jessica has a need to release her anger physically. How might we provide her with acceptable, non-harmful alternatives, rather than physical violence?

> **Jessica's mum despaired at her daughter's behaviour. She understood what was behind it, but as Jessica's younger sister Lisa took the brunt of the behaviour and was injured in the process, it was unacceptable.**
>
> **A friend of Mum's suggested buying a swing ball to divert the anger away from Lisa and on to something else.**
>
> **This was duly done. On returning home from school Jessica would disappear into the garden and spend ten minutes hitting the ball. She was able to release her aggression and tension in a non-harmful manner and it helped to reduce her after-school violence.**

Jessica was given an alternative form of behaviour that allowed her to release her aggression. Have a think about the types of physical behaviour that cause concern. Let's consider throwing. What alternatives could be put into place to allow the child a choice of how they could release anger that is non-threatening or dangerous?

- Throwing something that makes a noise (for example, plastic balls into metal bucket).
- Throwing something that changes (for example, throwing balls of play dough or plasticine on to a large floor target).
- Throwing paper aeroplanes (no damage can be caused).
- Throwing a ball outside (the rule is that the ball has to be retrieved each time it is thrown).
- Throwing punches at a balloon.

If behaviour is stopped at source the child has no way to release the emotion. The behaviour may escalate later as frustration builds. There are many techniques that employ encouraging alternative behaviour. These are explored later in the book.

If you are using replacement behaviour, always allow the child to release their aggression before expanding the idea into a learning activity. For instance, play dough target practice could evolve into a numeracy activity by adding up scores. The distance the play dough travelled could be added up or two children could compete against each other. This is fine to do, but after the child has released their aggression.

Chapter Two: Exploring challenging behaviour

All children and young people exhibit some behaviour that can be seen as challenging. How we address that behaviour depends on how damaging it may be. Is the behaviour damaging to the child, other children, yourself or property?

Let's look at two areas: **Dangerous** and **Non-Dangerous**

Consider the reasons why you are reading this book. The behaviours you are dealing with may clearly fall into one area or both.

The examples below illustrate the concept in relation to the behaviour being exhibited by Jack.

Dangerous Behaviour

- Violence to self, others and property
- Kicking
- Punching
- Biting
- Cutting
- Head Banging
- Lighting Fires
- Threatening behaviour

Both

- Sexual behaviour
- Bullying
- Running away
- Addictions – smoking, drinking, drugs
- Vandalism

Non-Dangerous Behaviour

- Making noises
- Swearing
- Answering back
- Being a drama queen
- Inappropriate body language

Think about this list. What would your priority be in managing Jack's behaviour? Would you want to stop or reduce the violence and sexual behaviours first? Obviously, it depends on the circumstance, but generally the choice will be affected by trying to keep others safe. It is impossible to deal with all behaviour at once. It is also important to recognise who may be at risk. By intervening, are you compromising your own safety?

© The Play Doctors Ltd.

We also need to consider intervention styles and approaches. How you intervene will affect how the individual responds, therefore affecting the outcome of the intervention.

The next graph takes a look at Leanne's behaviour.

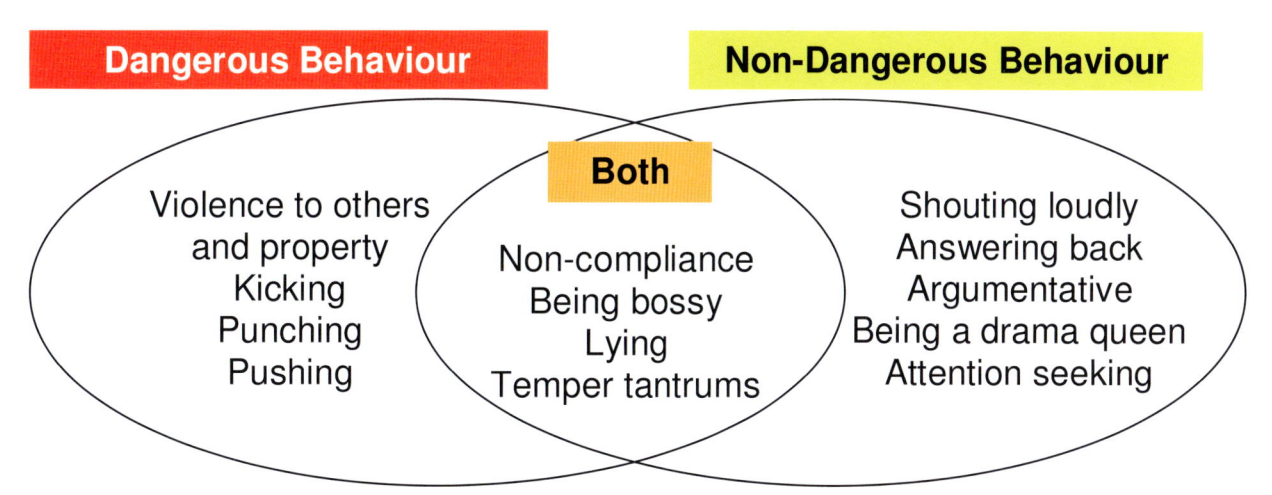

Dangerous Behaviour

Non-Dangerous Behaviour

Both

Violence to others and property
Kicking
Punching
Pushing

Non-compliance
Being bossy
Lying
Temper tantrums

Shouting loudly
Answering back
Argumentative
Being a drama queen
Attention seeking

When we look at the range of challenging behaviour, we need to decide which behaviours we want to concentrate on. Try choosing two or three key areas and focus on these first. Other improvements may happen after the key areas of behaviour have been changed. If we try to address all the behaviour issues at once, the child may feel that can never do anything right. So why try? By succeeding with small steps the child's confidence and self-esteem levels are raised, allowing progression in managing behaviour effectively. Other areas of the child's behaviour may improve without the need for further intervention.

Some socially unacceptable behaviour may escalate into dangerous behaviour. It is unusual for a child or young person to exhibit a single behaviour type; it is more usual to see a range of behaviours, for instance, swearing and poor body language, or swearing and violence.

Having suggested that we deal with the dangerous behaviour first, are we tolerating the non-dangerous or even giving approval via silence? The child still needs to behave within the rules or boundaries set. However, your focus and priority must be on changing dangerous behaviour. We often hear the phrase 'nipping it in the bud', meaning that we stop or resolve an issue before it escalates. This requires us to be vigilant, know our children and recognise potential triggers. Managing behaviour needs a whole setting or whole family approach, ensuring that our responses to behaviour are consistent, and agreement has been reached on which behaviours to concentrate on first.

> **Henry seems to be a very angry boy, often lashing out at other children, especially if they get in his way. He cannot understand the concept of waiting or taking turns.**
>
> **When he is frustrated he will shout and swear. Sometimes he will walk around repeating the same swear word over and over.**
>
> **When he gets angry he will head butt the nearest object, causing significant harm to himself and potentially others.**

Both sets of behaviour need supporting. Staff are more concerned about the self-harm. However, when this takes place in a childcare setting, parents are far more concerned about their own children hearing swear words. If the swearing is not dealt with, other children may feel the behaviour is acceptable, and will copy it. We need to balance and prioritise responses.

Henry's behaviour is taking place in a childcare setting. It is essential that the rules applied are there for all children and that 'special rules' are not given just for Henry.

Rules need to be owned by all children. If they are clearly involved in deciding what is acceptable and what is not acceptable there will be a level of self-policing.

The adult needs to ensure the rules are written in a positive manner. They may also suggest alternative ways of behaving to the children, for example, instead of 'no hitting', the rule may say: 'We are all friends here', or 'If you are angry you can draw on the angry board'.

Carole is 15; she has autism. She is generally very happy, co-operative and has never harmed another child. Carole hates shopping and is uncomfortable with people she does not know. She does not like loudspeaker systems as she cannot see who is speaking, and dislikes change.

Her mother has taken Carole to a large store to purchase new shoes. On entering the store, Carole feels anxious and, to calm herself, starts to hum.

Other shoppers glance over and look away. The shop tannoy system starts to make an announcement. Carole holds her hands over her ears, stands still and starts to hum more loudly. People now stop and stare. The store manager walks over to speak to mum...

What would you do if you were in mum's shoes? Is Carole doing anything to harm herself or others or is it just embarrassment that classes this type of behaviour as challenging?

Obviously, we don't know how predictable Carole may be or whether this behaviour is likely to escalate into a more dangerous situation. In the story, Carole is not causing harm to herself or others. Therefore, her behaviour is non-dangerous. However, at 15, Carole needs to learn and understand what is acceptable in public places and needs to be supported to modify her behaviour using alternative calming strategies.

Consider the following statements. Would you class this behaviour as challenging when exhibited in public places?

1. Swearing and shouting
2. Drinking alcohol in public
3. Kissing and cuddling in public
4. Flapping arms and spinning round in a circle
5. Kicking and biting
6. Throwing a temper tantrum and/or screaming

Your decision will be based against your own personal judgements. Some people will decide certain behaviour is acceptable or can be tolerated; others would want to change the behaviour being shown.

© The Play Doctors Ltd.

In Britain we often see young people outside, using the streets as a social environment. Some individuals class this as antisocial behaviour; others tolerate it. They recognise that the young people may have nowhere else to go or do not want to challenge behaviour because they feel threatened themselves. In some cultures, individuals are imprisoned for kissing in public; it is not accepted, tolerated or lawful.

A disabled child who flaps their hands and spins in a circle is seen as 'different', i.e. behaving in a way that conventional society deems socially unacceptable. Society judges the child to have challenging behaviour, rather than understand the underlying impairment and tolerating the behaviour. Perhaps it is society's thinking that needs challenging! Note here the use of the word 'conventional' rather than 'normal'. We are all different, so what is 'normal'?

If a child is behaving in a dangerous manner, the response: "He does not know what he is doing", therefore excusing the behaviour, is no excuse at all. We need to support children by initiating strong and appropriate communication, so that they can understand and respond to instruction and boundaries. This may require us to make adaptations to the ways in which we communicate. Make it appropriate to the individual child or young person, using augmented communication systems if necessary.

When an individual is stressed, communication skills are reduced. Children may hear an instruction but not realise it is directed at them. If we as adults are stressed when trying to support a challenging child, our own pitch and tone of voice change. This can add to the confusion. Remember to use the child's name so that they know the communication is directed towards them. Use short sentences and keep them to the point. If repeating sentences, use the same words. Get down to the child's level; otherwise you may seem threatening.

All children and young people want to explore boundaries from a very early age. Nyasha, aged 1, knows that it is wrong to touch the television remote control. However, after giving you a knowing look, she does it anyway. Why is this? Would you class it as a natural part of development and exploration of her environment, or a direct defiance of a parent's command?

This particular example is about Nyasha showing her independence. She knows she is not allowed to do it and, if there is no response from parents, she will do it again. If her parents give her boundaries and say "No" then she will learn that touching the television is 'out of bounds'.

Everyone uses a range of behaviour to express themselves or to communicate with others. Sometimes these behaviours are out of character, especially when we are angry, frustrated, cross, anxious, upset or fearful. We may feel like throwing something, or hitting out, but remain in control of our behaviour. We are able to regulate and have 'self-control'. This is what we need to teach children to use, by encouraging alternative ways to demonstrate our feelings. We also express behaviours differently when we are happy or excited. Can you remember the last time you actually jumped up and down with excitement?

Supporting children who are exhibiting challenging behaviour is not easy. Sometimes we cannot determine what the message is behind the behaviour, or understand what the child needs or wants. However, we need to take time out to observe and reflect on what went on. Then we can begin to establish an understanding of the behaviour being exhibited.

It is worth repeating the importance that the child or young person is NOT 'always in trouble'. If they feel that they can never do anything right, the young person may start believing that they cannot change the way they behave. Always criticise the behaviour and do not criticise the child or young person.

Behaviour is seen as far more challenging when the child or young person knows and understands what they are doing. Then the behaviour becomes the source of conflict. It does not always matter what the behaviour is; the resultant argument and response is, on occasion, the purpose behind the behaviour.

This is illustrated by Jack, who wants to have arguments. It is an opportunity for him to feel in control. At home Jack lacks the ability to have choice and control over his actions. His grandfather 'rules the roost', responding with violence. Jack tends to keep his head down.

Jack looks elsewhere to exert authority and feel big. He tends to pick on weaker people (not necessarily children) to win arguments. Jack does not necessarily think ahead to consider 'what will happen if'. He lives in the 'here and now' moment.

> On an estate within a small town, Jack hangs out with a group of young people aged 10 to 15. They tend to be out until about 11pm. There is a local park which is open to the elements, has no shelter from wind or rain and the gates are locked at 9pm. The young people choose to congregate behind the local shops in a block of garages. This is directly below a number of flats.
>
> During the evening the young people get cold and, to warm up, decide to light a fire. They are actually quite careful about this, choosing a safe place to light it on an apron of concrete away from the buildings. They collect a range of flammable materials such as wood and old furniture.
>
> Within ten minutes a local resident has seem flames and has called the fire brigade and police. The young people run away. However, they are very angry that their activities have been curtailed. A number of other small fires are lit over the next few weeks and a residents meeting takes place.
>
> Some residents understand the boredom the kids face and have suggested building a youth shelter in the park. Additionally, they thought the park should stay open later and a permanent, safe fire pit or barbeque area be built within the park. Others said how dangerous this would be and disagreed. They think the young people will set fire to the park, drink and take drugs, although there has been no evidence of this elsewhere.
>
> The young people themselves have not been invited to attend this meeting.

There are some questions that arise from this short story. We assume that the young people knew what they were doing, knew it would be seen as challenging behaviour, and yet did it anyway. Or, instead of planning to misbehave, were they identifying a solution to a problem? They were cold and wanted to get warm? How much blame do you put on the young people?

In this situation an argument ensued; not with the young people, but the local residents. Obviously, it was not appropriate to light a fire, and the residents were angry. However, again we look behind the behaviour to see what the communication tells us. Here, we recognise that the young people are bored. There is nothing to do and nowhere to go.

When we are dealing with behaviour that is seen as challenging, we need to ensure that our approach is agreed. If we set a range of differing boundaries, the child or young person will get confused and will not know what he is or is not allowed to do.

In this example, the local Police Community Support Officer (PSCO) was called in to liaise between the young people and the community. The first step was to listen to both sides, without judgement. This can be hard for us to do. We judge far too easily without necessarily knowing all the facts. We certainly do not always know how young people are feeling or what they actually want to happen.

There is an end to this story: the PSCO arranged several meetings between the residents and young people. Once the residents actually began to speak to the teenagers and have a two-way conversation, they realised that they were just young people with time on their hands and lots of energy. Negotiations were opened with the local council. It was agreed to open the park for longer hours. The PSCO supported the young people to write a proposal to the council to build two large, family brick barbeques on wasteland in the park.

The young people, alongside two residents and the PSCO, were involved in the planning and design. They met with the council to write a risk assessment and got involved in sourcing materials. A local builder's merchant donated bricks and mortar, and the project began. The fire brigade advised and also supported with building the structures.

Through this interaction the young people and residents got to know each other. The young people showed that they were capable of hard work and were willing to undertake something that was of benefit to them.

After the structures were built they were never vandalised. The young people were proud of their achievement and two even attended a food hygiene course so that they could cook a barbeque at a fun day in the park.

Of course, it was not as simple as it sounds; the project took a year to complete. There were various hurdles to cross including the response of the residents and the persuasion of the local parish council. Even after the project was completed several residents still felt it was the wrong thing to have done. Through the project, Jack's self-esteem and confidence levels were raised.

Put yourself in the position of Jack's grandparents at the beginning of this story. A PSCO comes knocking on the door to say that Jack had been lighting fires. Jack's grandmother felt powerless and did not know what to do or how to control Jack's behaviour.

His grandfather was very angry. Neither grandparent had the time or inclination to listen to Jack's side of the story. As far as they were concerned he had yet again displayed challenging behaviour. Jack's grandfather's initial reaction was to hit Jack. At some point Jack is likely to retaliate against his grandfather and hit him back.

Jack always felt that he was in trouble. Even when he tried to do the right thing people got the wrong end of the stick. His grandfather criticised him for working alongside the PCSO. He saw it as Jack being a traitor, working with the police.

Some residents constantly made comments and were forthcoming in their views of 'today's youth'. It took a lot of effort on the part of Jack and his mates to stick it out to the end; it would have been easier to forget the project. They needed praise and recognition each step of the way to succeed.

We also need to look for opportunities to praise and not criticise. Through this project, Jack's behaviour improved. He was not perfect by any means. However, the project taught him valuable skills such as: better communication; negotiation skills; and planning and conflict resolution. These will help him in the future.

We too can help children to develop these skills. Behaviour management is not all about stopping poor behaviour; it is about helping the child to develop strategies so they can choose alternative behaviours. Through our intervention and support children learn skills that are valuable throughout their lives.

Chapter Three:
Looking behind the behaviour

In the previous chapter we recognised that there is no clear definition of challenging behaviour. Behaviours that we perceive as challenging depend on the tolerance and understanding of the individual assessing them.

> **"Is this a phase they are going through?"** A question asked regularly by parents and guardians of disruptive children.
>
> **Is the behaviour part of growing up and becoming independent or is it part of life changes happening at the time?**
>
> **Is it a reflection of how others around them behave** or
>
> **Is it part of an underlying condition/impairment or does the child have a behavioural disorder?**

These are difficult questions and cannot be answered easily. Sometimes, it is necessary to request a formal assessment via the school or health service. Assessment can take many weeks. It will involve a range of people observing and recording the behaviour of the individual in different settings, at different times and when the child is with different people.

> **The teacher at Leanne's school writes a diary each day. Sometimes, Mum is afraid to read it. There are always issues recorded relating to Leanne's behaviour and Mum receives phone calls asking her to come into school to meet with the Head Teacher. This has caused her depression and anxiety.**
>
> **The school have suggested that Leanne undertakes a formal behavioural assessment. This will help the school to write an Individual Educational Plan known as an IEP. The IEP will also include a Behavioural Intervention Plan. Mum is actually quite glad that this is happening and it is relief to share her anxieties with someone else.**

An educational psychologist will be called in to begin the assessment. Generally the assessment is known as a Functional Behavioural Assessment (FBA) and will follow a strict formula.

Observations will be untaken by a number of staff including the teacher, teaching assistant, lunchtime supervisors and an educational psychologist (and other staff as appropriate). In addition, the student and parents will be asked for their thoughts. The key elements involved in this assessment are:
- A description of the behaviour being exhibited
- The setting in which the behaviour occurs, its frequency, intensity and duration
- The frequency of time outs or direct intervention
- The impact on the child's education
- The amount of work undertaken and grades of work
- A record of discipline referrals
- Structured observation

The assessment would then begin to dig a little deeper and ask further questions about the type of intervention used and responses. It will also look closely at the individual child, including any communication requirements. It will look at the wider context, including any family issues that may be affecting the behaviour of the child. Sometimes, the assessment will be part of the findings fed into a Common Assessment Framework (CAF). The CAF looks at how support can be offered to a family. It may be instigated by Social Services or another agency such as school or a health professional.

After the behaviour assessment has been made, an Intervention Plan will be written and put into place. This will indicate a range of interventions, what the expected outcomes are, who will be responsible and how reviews will take place. The assessment looks at more than the immediate behaviour. It is essential to take a look at the wider picture to see what is going on behind the behaviour.

We need to be aware that parents will respond to a request for an assessment in different ways. Some parents, such as Leanne's, are pleased that something is being done; others will not want an assessment to take place. They may feel threatened, that their parenting skills are being put under the spotlight and feel that they are being criticised. It is important to keep up a good relationship with parents/guardians and to ensure that any assessment is a positive and not a negative experience.

Of course, observations are not limited to just specialist services; we are all able to observe and try to make sense of what is happening. If a child you are working or living with already has a Behavioural Intervention Plan in place, it is important to ensure there is continuity of approach. The way you are responding to incidents should reflect the recommendations within the plan.

However, if a plan is not in place, there is no reason to stop you creating one of your own!

The plan still needs to involve a range of people, including the child or young person. Their involvement will obviously depend on their age. However, if we are trying to modify their behaviour, they will need to understand what, how and why.

On the next page we have provided a series of eight questions relating to the child's behaviour and background to the behaviour. They are designed to help you think about how to support the child or young person in your care. In this instance we have concentrated on play rather than education.

These are suggestions only and can be adapted according to your own situation and environment. Think 'outside the box' and put yourself into the child's mind. How do they see the same situation and what type of involvement should, and can, the child have in this observation?

Observation does not have to be obvious. Sitting with a clipboard can be very distracting for the child and will often cause them to modify their normal behaviour or 'act up' because they are being watched.

Consider how you can undertake unobtrusive observation and who might be involved. If you are working in a setting, much of the information will already be recorded in your normal records.

It will be necessary to carry out more than one observation. Children will behave in different ways all the time. We need to have an overview, rather than a one-off observation. Initial records will help to generate an action plan with further observations taking place to evaluate progress.

© The Play Doctors Ltd.

Suggested questions to include in an observational record

The notes below each question are to get you thinking and considering the broader picture.

1. Obvious questions such as date, day, time of day

When reviewing the observations you may find particular patterns, such as poor behaviour, happening regularly on a Monday. What happens on Mondays? Has the child had a poor weekend experience? Is the child facing a fear about returning to the setting? Has the child been at home or spent the weekend on an access visit? What do we know about the child's weekend and how this may have affected their behaviour?

Consider the time of day. Is the behaviour happening before lunch when the child is hungry? Or after lunch when the child has had something to eat? Is the behaviour affected by hunger or food intolerance such as sugar or colourant?

2. Description of behaviour(s)

It is unlikely that the child is only exhibiting one particular behaviour type; there are probably several key areas of concern. Record the types of behaviour the child is displaying. If these are numbered on your records it may be easier to record specific intervention styles for specific behaviours.

3. The setting in which the behaviour occurs

Consider the setting. Is the behaviour exhibited inside or outside, in a particular room or corridor or in the bathroom or toilets? Where does it tend to happen? Is there a pattern?

Also, have a think 'outside the box'. Is the behaviour being influenced by sensory stimulation? Is the setting particularly hot or cold? What kind of lighting is in the environment?

> **Jazel is very light sensitive. If the light is too dim he cannot see well and he gets bad headaches when lights flicker. Jazel has difficultly in expressing how he is feeling and if the light is annoying him he tends to take it out on others. His behaviour includes pushing in, taking toys from others and arguing.**
>
> **He prefers natural light and chooses to play with other children in front of the large patio windows. He will move toys into the light, rather than move himself over to the toys. Recently, he was caught trying to pull the large sand tray and contents to the patio windows.**

What could you do to help Jazel and reduce poor behaviour?

4. When does the behaviour occur?

This question looks at both the frequency of the behaviour and links to the record of the timing of the behaviour. Again, are there any patterns emerging? Does the behaviour happen just before home time? If so, what is happening when the child is collected? Does the behaviour happen after the child has visited the toilet? Are they constipated and uncomfortable? Do they need the toilet when the behaviour occurs?

5. Who is involved?

Does the behaviour only occur with certain individuals?

Christopher is on the autism spectrum. He enjoys being in his play setting and likes his personal play worker. However, on occasion he would try to attack her, tearing at her clothes.

During observation it was noted that this behaviour only took place on the days the play worker wore a specific red fleece. Christopher could not abide the colour red as it created a sensory overload.

Through observation and records the reason behind this behaviour was discovered. The play worker stopped wearing a red fleece and Christopher no longer attacked her. Staff in the setting were aware of the need to reduce colour stimulation, particularly in relation to the colour red.

We have all been in situations where we need to separate groups of children. We may also need to engineer opportunities for children to play together working towards a joint aim to increase social interaction and tolerance of each other.

Is the challenging behaviour being modelled by other children and young people? Who are they copying the behaviour from, and why?

Have a think about how the adult dealing with the incident is behaving. Are they displaying anger, frustration, fear, anxiety or are they calm, using clear simple language and using the child's name? Be honest in your assessment. How an adult responds will affect the child's response, for example, if the adult raises their voice the child may feel they have been given permission to shout.

> Emma is a 2 year old, attending a local pre-school. When she first started at the setting she did not want her mum to leave. She recognised that whenever she went to anyone wearing a blue T-shirt, her mum would leave. Consequently, she learned not to go near anyone wearing the setting uniform and would scream if anyone wearing a blue T-shirt approached.
>
> Staff observed this behaviour and made sure that, when they met her and welcomed her into the setting, they wore cardigans or jumpers over their uniform. Emma was then quite happy to be with them.
>
> Once she had got used to the staff and setting, she was very happy for her mum to leave. The behaviour was supported through observation and adaptation to address Emma's fears.

By asking someone else to observe a child's behaviour it is possible to record not only who is dealing with the situation but also how they are reacting. What else is going on in the room verbally and non-verbally?

Ensure that the person who is undertaking the observation does not get involved. As soon as you are involved it is impossible to record objectively.

6. What are the consequences of the behaviour?

Describe previous interventions and what sanctions are being imposed. What has happened as the result of the behaviour? How has the child responded? Think back and check any notes you have made.

Have threats been made and not carried out?
Has the sanction been too great for the behaviour?
Was the sanction relevant to the child?
Has the consequence happened immediately or is there a delay in responding to behaviour?

These questions require a level of honest self-reflection. It is easy to concentrate on the child's behaviour and not so easy to assess our own!

> **Henry hates maths; he finds it difficult to concentrate and gets distracted very easily. He uses avoidance tactics to get out of uncomfortable situations. During maths he will constantly move around the classroom, make noises, pick up other children's work and generally behave in an unacceptable way.**
>
> **For the sake of the rest of the children, the class teacher asks the teaching assistant to take Henry out of class into the playroom. The theory is that the lesson will continue on a one-to-one basis between Henry and the teaching assistant. However, the playroom is far too exciting and Henry is happy getting toys out of cupboards. He will not listen to the teaching assistant. He has achieved his goal, which is:**
>
> - **To move out of the classroom**
> - **To avoid the work he is being asked to do**
> - **To have one-to-one attention**
> - **To be in the playroom**

What is the payback from the behaviour? Does the child get what they want by behaving in that way? When considering sanctions, think about what the child wants to achieve. If the benefits are taken away or reduced the child may wonder if the behaviour is worth it. Consequences and sanctions are discussed in more detail later in the book.

7. Is there an underlying condition, impairment or external issues affecting the behaviour?

Two of the short case studies used in this section so far have illustrated behaviour being exhibited which relates to an underlying impairment. We need to adapt our work to support specific requirements, but we must also ensure all children still abide by the setting or house rules. Our adaptations may be in the way we communicate those house rules effectively to ensure all children understand what is acceptable.

Is there anything happening in the child or young person's life that may affect their behaviour? Family issues, changes of circumstance or bereavement may mean that you are seeing temporary changes in behaviour patterns. It may not be possible to address those issues, but understanding them may influence how the behaviour is managed. The knowledge will require you to consider how specific support is provided to the child or young person and, if appropriate, their family.

If a behavioural disorder has been formally diagnosed a number of people may require support. Consider the impact on the immediate family, including siblings. Think about what your role is in relation to support. If you are the one working with the child, how are you receiving support yourself? If you are the parent/guardian or a lone worker, you may wish to research support networks in your own area. Talking to other parents and professionals experiencing similar situations can be helpful.

8. Are you aware of any messages being given through the behaviour?

Have you already considered the messages behind the behaviour? If so, what have you picked up? In the examples given we have learnt:

- Jazel finds working or playing in dim light difficult. Some lights may be too bright and flickering lights cause him headaches. When he gets headaches he will display challenging behaviour towards others.
- Christopher has sensory sensitivities, particularly in relation to the colour red. He feels more secure in a low arousal atmosphere. High arousal environments may trigger a violent outburst.
- Henry has decided to use a behaviour strategy to get what he wants. The communication is 'I hate maths and want out of here'.
- Emma has learnt to avoid blue uniforms so that Mum does not leave.

Once you have begun to assess the observations, the reasons behind the behaviour may become clearer. This may influence your response. All strategies and interventions need to ensure messages are clear and that children understand the boundaries and rules. They should know what their choices are and that if sanctions are given they will be carried out.

It is likely that you already have boundaries in place for the children in your care. It is important to ensure these are consistent across all settings. Children and young people will become confused if they are allowed to behave in certain ways at one setting but not at another.

Some children find transition very difficult. If an after school club is happening in the school that the children attend, they may become confused if there are two sets of rules. This could be as simple as the child having to ask permission to use the toilet at school. The after school club may encourage the child to go on their own, supporting independence.

> **A youth group had a rule that there would be no teasing or bullying.**
>
> Sharmain was sitting to one side during a discussion group at the youth club. The group were trying to decide where they wanted to go for a trip out. The group were all interested and paying attention. However, Sharmain was tapping a pencil on the side of her chair, yawning and looking at her watch.
>
> Previously during the session she had picked on one of the younger kids. Sharmain had teased her about having plaits and offered to cut her hair short, which had upset the girl.
>
> The youth worker who was talking looked down at his notes. During that split second Sharmain threw a rubber across the room towards the girl she had been teasing. The rubber hit her in the eye. It was unexpected; the girl was surprised and fell off her seat.
>
> At this point Sharmain laughed loudly. The youth worker subsequently banned her from going on the trip.

The sanction imposed sounds effective. However, the reality is that Sharmain was in a bad mood because she knew she would not be able to go on the trip. She would not ask her foster parents for money and she had very little money of her own. The youth worker knew of her situation and that it was unlikely she would attend. Do you think this was an effective sanction?

What would you have done in this situation? Perhaps the youth worker was displaying understanding by eliminating Sharmain's embarrassment that she would not be attending the trip, but at the same time being seen to address the bullying that was going on. Do you feel that the sanction was fair and will have any effect on Sharmain?

If the youth worker knew Sharmain would have difficulty paying for the trip, perhaps he should have quietly addressed this with her before the group discussion. This may have eliminated her bad temper or changed the way he gave the details about the trip to the group.

Let's put this observational learning into context
To put this learning into context we have completed a short observation of Henry. As you read through this, consider the comments. Decide what you would put into place, and how.

Henry's story: background

Cherry Trees is an after school club offering childcare to children aged between 4 and 15 years. The club is based in the local primary school, although children from other schools also attend. The club has a regular attendance of twenty-five children and five staff members. Out of the children attending, eight are aged between 4 and 6 years, thirteen are aged between 7 and 11 years and the remaining four are aged between 12 and 15 years.

The club offers a range of activities such as arts/crafts, games and a quiet area where children are encouraged to complete their homework. The outdoor play area is available to use, so long as the weather is good. A number of outdoor activities are provided such as balls, bats, skipping ropes and the static play equipment used by the school.

At the local after school club Henry has been displaying challenging behaviour. The manager of the setting and the play workers are concerned. This is affecting their relationship with him and his relationship with other children. They are on the verge of excluding him.

The club is based in the school Henry attends. The manager has had an informal conversation with Henry's teacher. Henry is known in school to have ADHD. He will disrupt lessons and occasionally get violent. He finds it difficult to concentrate. Henry's teacher has shared some behavioural strategies with the after school club. These are based around short key tasks, structure and sequence. They are not necessarily appropriate to the informality of the play setting.

The staff team decide that they need to make an informal observation. They want to find out what is happening, and try to work out what they can put into place to support Henry, who is obviously unhappy and angry.

The setting manager decided that she would like to do this observation herself.

Cherry Trees Behavioural Observation Record

1. Observation Record

Record taken by: Jacky – Manager
Date of observation: 16th May
Day of the week: Tuesday
Time of day: 3.30-6.00pm

2. Description of behaviour observed

a. Lack of engagement in play
b. Flitting from one activity to another
c. Throwing activities on the floor
d. Taking toys away from younger children
e. Laughing when younger children cry
f. Running away from play workers when they ask him to stop. (Favourite place to run is behind the shed in the playground)
g. Answering adults back
h. Constant loud repetition of the same swear word
i. Hitting play worker with plastic bat

3. The setting in which the behaviour occurs

Behaviour observed in most areas of the room used. Behaviour did not occur in the quiet area or where the older children were using the computer. The majority of behaviour occurred at the crafts table and outside in the play area. Argument between staff member and Henry occurred in the playground, out of sight, behind the shed.

4. When does the behaviour occur?

Henry came into the club at 3.30pm. The first behaviour recorded was at 3.35pm. Henry moved between three activity tables and at each table swept something from the table onto the floor, refusing to pick it up when asked. Becky, a play worker, told him that if his behaviour had not improved he would not get a snack.

Behaviour improved at 4pm, prior to snack time. Henry was compliant and offered to help. Henry is aware that he will not get a snack if he does not line up nicely with the other children. He is always first in line, waiting five minutes before the snack bar opens.

The incident of running outside occurred at 4.30pm after Henry had eaten a chocolate bar and a banana. Henry was standing by the older children and started to repeat a particular swear word over and over. Becky, a play worker, tried to address this behaviour and asked him to stop swearing. Henry ran outside and hid behind the shed.

© The Play Doctors Ltd.

Becky tried to get him back inside. This was done through encouragement, bribery and eventually threats. Henry would not comply, swore, picked up a plastic bat, swung it and hit Becky in the face. This situation ended up with Becky in tears. At this point, I intervened, sent Becky to the staffroom and told Henry that he had to come inside.

Henry complied and played for a while with the sand tray. Other children who were playing with the sand moved on to other activities, leaving Henry to play on his own.

5.15pm Henry was asked if he needed the toilet. He said no, but at 5.20pm went to the toilet and remained there for ten minutes. At 5.30pm a play worker went to check if he was okay. Henry was fine and came back into the room.

At this point, I told Henry he had to apologise to Becky. He did so, grudgingly. From 5.30pm until 5.50pm, his behaviour improved. He went to Becky, the play worker he had hit, and asked if she would play with him. They took a football outside and had a kick around for ten minutes, followed by Becky reading him a book.

At 5.50pm Henry fetched his coat and bag and stood next to the door waiting for his mum to collect him at 6pm. As Mum arrived, Henry immediately ran out to the car, leaving no time for Mum to speak to staff members.

5. Who is involved?
<ul><li>Other children, particularly younger children who are easy to upset</li><li>Older children were not the focus of Henry's attention</li><li>All staff members, particularly Becky</li><li>Myself as manager</li></ul>
6. What are the consequences of the behaviour?
<ul><li>Henry was told he needed to improve his behaviour or he would not get a snack</li><li>Henry knew that if I said he had to go back inside, I meant it</li></ul>

> **7. Is there an underlying condition, impairment or external issue affecting behaviour?**
> - Yes, we know that Henry has ADHD. He cannot help some of his behaviour
> - We have difficulty in talking to Mum as she needs to leave immediately with Henry when she collects him
> - His behaviour is poor at school, but worse at after school club
>
> **8. Are you aware of any messages being given through the behaviour?**
> - Henry is bored?
> - He does not like the staff members?
> - Henry will behave when he wants something (snack time)
> - Henry does not want to be at after school club; he wants to be at home
> - Henry's behaviour improved after he went to the toilet

After the observation took place, Jacky and her staff sat down to consider what had been learnt. They discussed how they could use this information to create an action plan to support Henry's behaviour. During this meeting several interesting things emerged.

The discussion followed the themes of the observation:

Description of behaviour
All staff agreed with the description of behaviour that was recorded. Staff also gave the following thoughts:

- There are too many choices for Henry to cope with all at once.
- No activity planning had taken place to specifically consider Henry's personal likes and dislikes.
- He tends to focus any bullying on younger children where he gets a response. This initiates attention of play workers.
- He seems to find the response of his behaviour funny, laughing when a younger child cries.
- He seems to enjoy 'the chase' when he runs away.
- By answering an adult back, he initiates an argument or reaction.

© The Play Doctors Ltd.

- He enjoys the attention given by swearing.
- Sometimes the swearing seems to be a habit, rather than a designed behaviour.
- He uses violence as a strategy to get out of a situation. He does not seem to know or understand that other strategies are available.

The setting in which the behaviour occurs
- Henry enjoys secret places, out of sight of others. Staff suggested this may because he can cut down sensory stimulation. He can be in a place where he does not have to respond to other children and enjoys his own company.
- Much of the poor behaviour was based around the craft table. Henry does not enjoy crafts. He lacks imagination and finds creative play difficult and pointless.
- Henry enjoys being outside where he is not confined and able to move freely.

When does the behaviour occur?
- Immediately. Staff felt that he was overwhelmed as soon entering the room.
- Behaviour improved before snack time. Proof that he can control his behaviour when he gets something he wants.
- Physically challenging behaviour starts after snack time. Staff observed that he had eaten chocolate and wondered whether behaviour was related to a sugar rush.
- The swearing started after he had been near the older children. One staff member reported that earlier in the session she had spoken to these children about swearing. Staff wondered if Henry's swearing was related to copied behaviour that was being modelled by the older children.
- Henry needed the toilet but had either not recognised the feeling or had forgotten to go. Staff felt that he was actually quite uncomfortable, which may have affected his behaviour. Henry eventually apologised to Becky after going to the toilet and at this point his behaviour improved.
- Henry was obviously clock watching, being ready and waiting for his mum to collect him. Staff were unsure if this was because Henry did not want Mum speaking to staff, or if he just 'wanted out of there'.

Who is involved?
- Staff discussed how Becky had tried to persuade Henry to come back into the building. Becky reported that she had initially tried to encourage Henry back in by offering to play with him. As Henry continued to swear and answer back, Becky's response was to tell Henry he was being silly, and it was not surprising that he had no friends. She also said that if he did not come back in he would have no snack the following day. Becky felt that she had no or little support from other staff members in this instance.
- It was noted that Henry did not display challenging behaviour to provoke older children, but focused attention on younger children.
- Henry seemed to respond better on a one-to-one basis, where he had the attention of one play worker. Henry was happy to forget his poor behaviour relating to Becky when he played with her later in the session.
- Jacky was seen by Henry to be a voice of authority, going inside when she told him to. It was noted that this may have been because Becky cried and Henry realised that he had overstepped the mark.

What are the consequences of the behaviour?
- After discussion, staff realised that actually there was very little in the form of consequences that would have been meaningful to Henry. The threat of not having a snack was given twice. In the session Henry then behaved for a short period to 'get what he wanted' and the second threat related to not having a snack the following day. This was too far ahead for Henry to worry about.
- Henry realised that, if he behaved badly, he would get the attention of play workers and may have a play worker all to himself for a while.

Is there an underlying condition, impairment or external issue affecting behaviour?
- Staff decided that they were making too many allowances for Henry's impairment. There seemed to be two rules: one for Henry and one for the rest of the children.
- Staff also realised that they knew very little about his background, his family situation, how his mother coped with his behaviour and what types of strategies were used at home. Staff also wanted to know if any changes had taken place to affect Henry's behaviour, for example, bereavement, illness in the family, changes to circumstance.

Lastly, the team discussed consequences of behaviour. There were many differing views about: time out; sanctions; punishments; children being told off; and children's ability to re-earn privileges if behaviour improved.

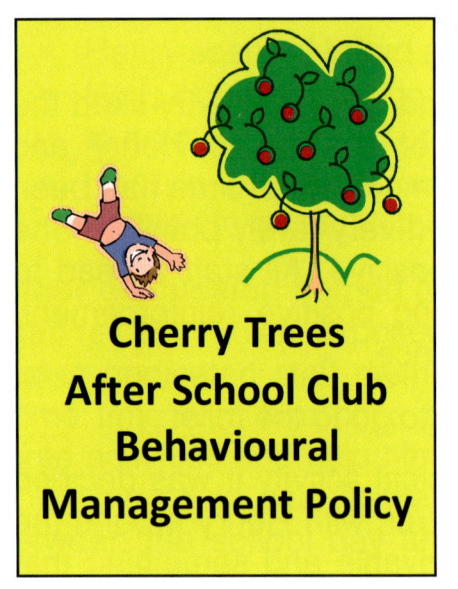

Cherry Trees After School Club Behavioural Management Policy

Jacky decided that this was a bigger subject and they needed to consider a setting behavioural management policy for the whole after school club. A meeting was set to discuss it further.

The team agreed that the way forward for Henry was to create a SMART action plan. Actions and targets always need to be Specific, Measurable, Achievable, Realistic and Timely. This needed to involve everybody, including Henry himself, a conversation with Mum and a further chat with his teacher.

How an action plan is drawn up is up to you and the setting in which you work. It needs to be clear and provide actions that can be measured to see if the plan is making a difference. Identify who, what, when and how. The plan needs to have regular review dates to check on progress and make any changes as necessary.

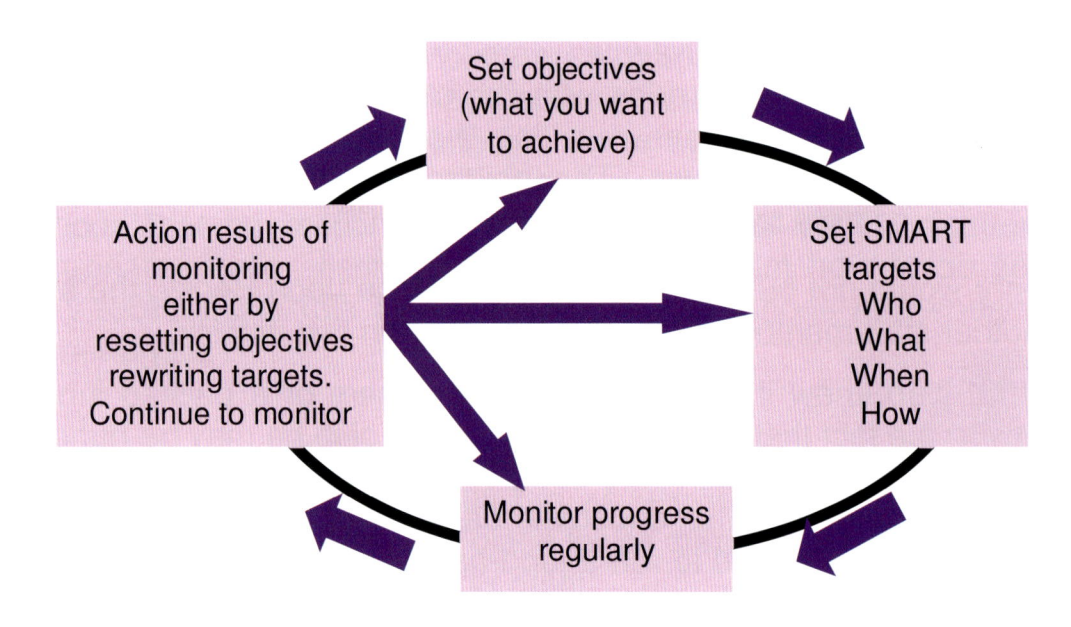

- Set objectives (what you want to achieve)
- Set SMART targets: Who, What, When, How
- Monitor progress regularly
- Action results of monitoring either by resetting objectives rewriting targets. Continue to monitor

© The Play Doctors Ltd.

Considering Henry's Action Plan

Who
- **Henry** needs to understand appropriate behaviour and be given alternative acceptable behaviour to release his aggression.
- **All children** in the setting need to re-establish agreed rules.
- **All staff** in the setting need to know who is taking the lead on what area and ensure that there is a consistency of approach from all staff.
- **Henry's teacher** needs to be 'in the loop'.
- **The family** need to be engaged. Some strategies may be planned to work both at home, at school and at the setting.

What
- The plan will identify specific actions.
    - Some actions will relate to the type of response given to Henry's behaviour
    - Some will be preventative measures (including the clear setting of boundaries and rules). Some will reduce over stimulation and empower play by restricting choice (offering two or three alternatives for Henry to choose from)
    - Some will be offering Henry acceptable alternative behaviour

When
- In addition to identifying short-, medium- and long-term goals, it is important to identify when strategies and techniques will be put into place: before, during and after an incident. This includes when sanctions (if used) will be actioned.

How
- The strategies need to be agreed and remain consistent.
- Regular monitoring to take place through observations, records and discussion. Don't forget to involve Henry. As his behaviour improves, praise is given, his self-esteem and confidence will rise and he should begin to feel better about himself.
- Consideration needs to be given as to how the strategies are to be implemented. For instance, some children will respond far better to visual stimuli and visual cues. Too much language is overwhelming.

So far, this chapter has primarily focused on one particular case study. However, the learning is appropriate to all situations.

If you are working with younger children, remember they may have not yet learned how to react to feelings and needs in an acceptable way. Our role is to support them to understand appropriate ways to behave and teach them skills for life.

In younger children we need to remember that:
- Behaviour is learnt by copying others.
- Behaviour can change as acceptable ways of behaving are taught.
- Practice makes perfect – we don't get it right all the time (both children and the way we respond to the challenges).
- Rewards work better than punishments (children will work towards receiving something they want and may display more challenging behaviour as a result of a sanction).
- Consistency is the key (ensure we are always responding in the same way).

We cannot assume that a child always misbehaves intentionally. We need to look at what happens after the child has misbehaved to establish the consequences. If a young child has a 'paddy' because they cannot have something they want, and the adult gives in due to embarrassment or frustration, of course the child will misbehave in the same way again. They have learnt that this is how they need to behave to get something they want.

If the child has not been given acceptable alternatives, or does not know how else to behave, they will continue the same behaviour. Very young children have not yet learnt what appropriate behaviour is. We need to tell them clearly and kindly, focusing on what we want them to do rather than what we don't want them to do.

We, as adults, have a responsibility to model behaviour and show respect to the children in our care. We expect the children to abide by sets of rules. We need to set ourselves some clear guidelines. Ask yourself (and be honest):
- How do we actively listen to children?
- What type of language are we using, including facial expressions, body posture, the way we talk and the way we touch?
- What is the quality of the attention we give to the child?
- What messages are we giving and receiving?

It is easy to observe and judge the child; it is harder to take a step back and observe ourselves. Reflective practice is important to understand our own role in influencing how a situation escalates or diminishes.

© The Play Doctors Ltd.

The local primary school was experiencing difficulties during lunchtime periods. The supervisors were regularly sending between six and eight children to the Head's office each day for poor behaviour.

The children were shouting, fighting, swearing and arguing. When asked what training would help, one supervisor said: "Crowd control!" During observation, the following was identified:
- Children were bored. School equipment was not allowed to be used at lunchtimes. Some children brought in their own activities.
- There were no playground rules.
- The supervisors were not respected as they were known to the children out of school.
- The playground itself had very poor marking, which caused confusion. Children wanting to play football did not have any defined area. This meant that other children were constantly wandering into their game.
- There were lots of hidden areas where children felt unsafe from bullies.

The school decided to put a 'play at playtime' project into place. After consultation with the children they purchased some play equipment. Children were supported to set up and manage a lunchtime equipment library. The playground was re-marked by volunteers defining areas designed by the children. A friendship bench was purchased and friendship mentors recruited. Playground rules were written and agreed with the children.

Logs were placed around the outside of the hardstanding, allowing children to sit and watch football. The supervisors were provided with bright yellow fleeces, giving them a sense of belonging and allowing children to recognise who was in authority during lunchtimes. Finally, the supervisors' job descriptions were changed to 'Lunchtime Play Workers'.

After the changes were made and implemented there was a significant reduction in poor behaviour. Supervisors sent very few children to the Head's office and children reported increased enjoyment and a reduction in the fear of bullying.

© The Play Doctors Ltd.

Chapter Four: Setting the boundaries

We now start to broaden our thinking and explore ideas behind setting effective boundaries.

How do you primarily communicate with children?
You may wonder why we are asking this question at the beginning of a chapter on setting the boundaries. However, there is a great deal to be said about how we set boundaries through our own communication. Children and young people will copy, imitate, and respond in kind to our own overtures. Communication may be verbal and non-verbal.

When we

- raise our voice;
- swear;
- use poor body language;
- refuse to listen;
- do not pay attention;
- pretend to listen;
- base our listening on past behaviour;
- jump ahead when listening and assume;

we give permission to the children to do the same. We can destroy our own boundaries and rules in a fraction of a second.

We ourselves act as a positive or negative influence. This is interpreted by children through the way we communicate. By providing a positive influence, we are setting our own standards and boundaries. We expect the children to act in the way we role model behaviour.

It is easy to say and not so easy to do. When we are dealing with a difficult situation, we need to concentrate hard to ensure we are keeping a nice, easy, friendly but firm tone of voice. We need to be consistent in our messages and use appropriate body language: firm yet still open; definitely not closed or negative.

It is hard not to judge and base our understanding on previous behaviours. When managing behaviour, it is important to only deal with the current situation. Don't use accusatory language or focus on past misdemeanours.

Positive and negative cycles of influence

Let's give this some context. If an adult displays positive feelings and words to a child or young person, they tend to respond in kind. The child enjoys recognition and praise and feels good about themselves. They end up wanting more of the same because they enjoy the attention.

Because they want more praise and possibly rewards, the children behave positively to achieve their aim. Consequently this results in more praise being given by the adult, more good feelings by the child, and creates a cycle of positive influence.

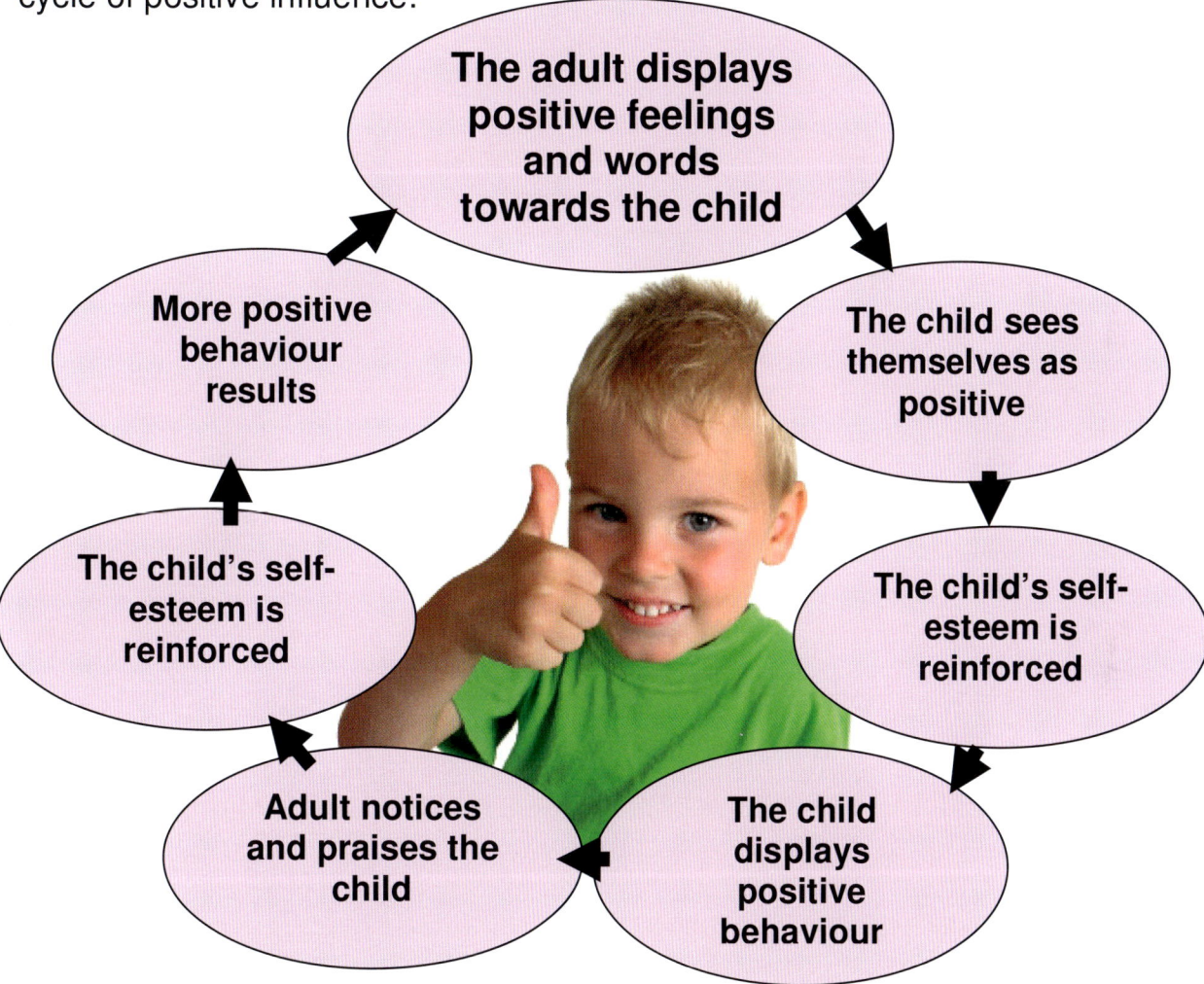

- The adult displays positive feelings and words towards the child
- The child sees themselves as positive
- The child's self-esteem is reinforced
- The child displays positive behaviour
- Adult notices and praises the child
- The child's self-esteem is reinforced
- More positive behaviour results

Remember, children respond to praise in different ways. Some children, (particularly those with social communication impairments) will not respond to social praise. It may not be tangible or have a meaning. Instead, try using a simple reward system such as stickers and positive body language. It may be more beneficial to allow the child five minutes to play with their favourite activity. Make the praise appropriate for the individual child or young person.

> **Sharmain went to make herself a cup of tea. Her little one-year-old foster sister, Nyasha, held her hands out to take the hot mug, indicating that she wanted a drink. Without being asked, Sharmain went back into the kitchen and made her a milky cup of tea in a Sippy cup.**
>
> **Linda, Sharmain's foster mum, saw what she had done and thanked her. She also added that she was really pleased with how Sharmain looked after Nyasha, and said: "You know, there are very few people I would trust to look after Nyasha, but you are one of them."**
>
> **Sharmain felt good about this and could not help offering a little smile. She was proud that she could be trusted. Linda noticed the smile and decided to back up her words with an action. She would normally ask Sharmain to go to the corner shop and fetch some milk. However, this time she asked Sharmain if she would be willing to babysit for a few minutes while she went to the shop.**
>
> **This was a rare occurrence in Sharmain's life; to be trusted like this with a child who needed her. Sharmain, unusually, agreed without an argument.**
>
> **When Linda returned from the shops, Nyasha was sitting on Sharmain's lap and they were playing peek-a-boo together. Linda smiled at Sharmain and, for the first time, got a real smile back.**

The reward Sharmain received for her behaviour was to be given responsibility. This raised her self-esteem and confidence, and she felt she was trusted. The incident built on her relationship with both Nyasha and her stepmum.

Linda could have just thanked her and left it at that. Although Sharmain would accept the thanks, it would probably have been with a shrug of the shoulders, and no further interaction would have taken place.

Consider how you can build on small steps to create a cycle of positive influence with children and young people. Catch them doing something good!

© The Play Doctors Ltd.

What happens when the opposite occurs?

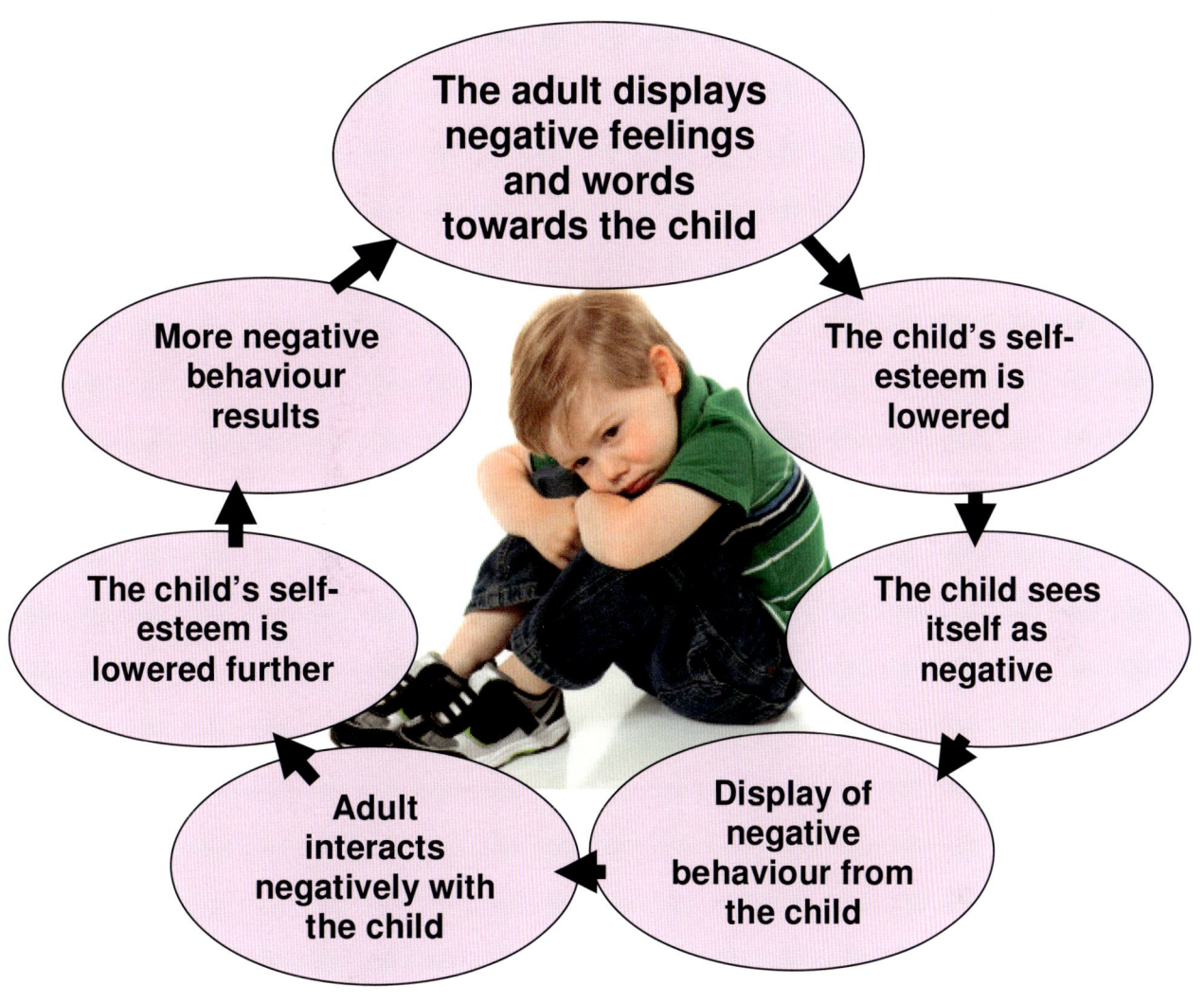

- The adult displays negative feelings and words towards the child
- The child's self-esteem is lowered
- The child sees itself as negative
- Display of negative behaviour from the child
- Adult interacts negatively with the child
- The child's self-esteem is lowered further
- More negative behaviour results

It is all too easy to respond in kind. When we are dealing with a challenging situation, our own emotions are high. We may find ourselves rising to the bait, and reflecting the child's behaviour, even when we are trying not to.

Have a look at the following conversations.

Conversation 1: The play worker notices a child just about to kick another...

"You know you must not kick, you are being very naughty."
"I want to kick."
"That's naughty; I don't like you when you kick."
"Well, I don't like you either."
"That's not a nice thing to say."
"You said it to me!"

During the first conversation the play worker is accusatory, directing her feelings towards the child rather than the behaviour. The conversation is spiralling into a negative cycle of influence.

Conversation 2

"Let's keep our feet on the ground."
"I want to kick."
"I know. I have seen you kick a football really well. Hey, let's go and find a football to kick."
"I want to kick Ben."
"It will hurt Ben if you kick him. Do you like being hurt?"
"No, I don't like being hurt."
"No, Ben does not like being hurt either. Shall we kick something that will not hurt?"
"Okay."
"Let's say sorry to Ben first, before we go and play football."
"Sorry, Ben."

During the first part of the conversation the play worker is giving a positive instruction 'feet on the ground' rather than a negative 'don't kick'.

This instruction is in itself a boundary. The play setting displays some positive rules including 'We keep our feet on the ground'.

During the second part of the conversation the play worker recognises that the child wants to kick. She looks for both an alternative behaviour and an opportunity to praise the child.

The play worker explains to the child what will happen if the child kicks Ben – it will hurt Ben. The play worker decides not to move into a negative conversation by saying what sanctions will be given to the child if he kicks Ben. This would be negative and could be used later if the child does not decide to make a better choice. Provide a choice by offering an alternative form of behaviour. If the child chooses to continue the unacceptable behaviour then the choice includes the sanction.

The play worker asks the child if they would want the same thing to happen to them. The child states they would not want to be kicked. The offer of alternative behaviour is made again. The child now wants to play with the play worker and is happy to say sorry to Ben.

© The Play Doctors Ltd.

Ben's feelings also need to be taken into consideration. He could also be invited to play football or offered something else he enjoys doing.

Here, the play worker has broken the negative cycle of influence and has begun to change the direction of behaviour.

This illustration may seem simple. Life throws us the unexpected. We need to respond quickly to situations and often have little time to plan what we say and how we respond.

It is important to recognise how quickly we are responding. We sometimes respond with little thought and take too little time to consider. Have we recognised the feelings of the other party? What could be an alternative acceptable behaviour?

> **Leanne was having a bad day. It had started off badly when the cereal she wanted had run out; she had to have a different sort. This put her into a bad temper. She told her mum, Jan, that she was a bad mum, not providing for her children!**
>
> **The comment irritated Jan. She responded by reminding Leanne that it was her fault that they had not gone to the supermarket the previous evening because Leanne had been naughty.**
>
> **This made Leanne even crosser. She ended up throwing the cereal bowl across the kitchen. Jan stood up, leaned over Leanne and told her to go to her room and get ready for school. Leanne went to kick her mother, who then swore at her. This gave Leanne permission to swear back. On being told not to swear, she responded by saying: "Well, you did!"**

It's easy to judge when we read this story. Perhaps it is not easy to be in that situation. How could Jan have reacted differently to reduce Leanne's anger?

Let's replay...
Initially, Leanne was not offered any alternatives for breakfast. As the cereal had run out, Jan told her she had to have something she did not like. Understandably, providing choice at this point may have caused Jan more work.

However, Jan could have said: "Morning you. We've run out of Weetabix. We've got bread for toast or Frosties. What would you like?"

The choice may be limited, but Leanne kept a level of control. She could decide what she would like. This simple start may have eliminated the ensuing argument.

What could happen if Leanne still wants to argue and accuse her mum of not providing for her children? In the story, Mum begins to replay the previous evening, blaming Leanne for the lack of cereal. Perhaps Mum could have responded differently. Fetching a pen and paper she could say: "Okay, let's make a shopping list. What do we need?"

When Leanne threw the cereal bowl across the room, Mum's response was anger. However, did you notice that no sanction had been put into place? Asking Leanne to go to her room and get ready for school was not a punishment. She had to do that anyway. Leanne may not have wanted to be in her room. However, once there, she would be able to play with her own toys and activities and do what she wanted.

Mum could have said: "We eat nicely in this house. If you don't eat nicely then you know what happens..."

It seems that Leanne has little in the form of boundaries. If she lived in a home where rules were clear and consistent, she would know what happens.

Non-compliance or poor behaviour may mean a time out period or other sanction. Sanctions need to be relevant and appropriate. These are discussed later in the book.

What happens when a child or young person is always negative? They constantly put themselves down or just won't try to do anything? The negative cycle still needs to be broken. The child's self-esteem and confidence levels are likely to be very low.

Try to record positive aspects of the child's day. Use a camera (with permission) to take shots of things the child enjoys doing. Catch them being good in order to praise them. Ask them to record what went well. Provide them with a sticker to go into their picture diary.

© The Play Doctors Ltd.

Ask them what most pleased them about their day. Tell them something that pleased you about their behaviour. If possible, try to do this in front of someone, perhaps the child's parents or guardian so that the praise turns into raised self-esteem.

Recognise the way the child is feeling but do not let negativity rule. If this is allowed it can turn into depression and mental health issues. Ask yourself if the negativity is actually attention seeking. If you feel it is, look for other ways to provide attention. Support the child to undertake hobbies that can be praised. These do not need to be complicated.

If a child is feeling negative about themselves, get other children to think of positive things about them.

> **Kate felt bad. She was disappointed in herself and did not feel that she was good at anything. She looked at Nicole's work and thought it was better than hers. She saw Sied's 'well done' sticker and felt she would never be given one.**
>
> **Kate's teacher noticed. She asked all the children to write one thing they especially liked about each other on to paper flower petals. Each child was given their personal flower. Kate realised that the other children actually liked her and thought she**

Remember that sometimes we all need time and space to 'sound off'. We may resent being 'jollied along', and find it frustrating. Know your own children and what is right for them. Don't forget the value of walking, talking and listening.

Monologue or dialogue?

In the previous examples we have illustrated both monologue, where the adult is talking at the child, and dialogue, where a two-way conversation is invited.

Think of a recent conversation you have had with a child or young person. What went well, and why? What did not go quite so well?

We asked a number of adults the same questions. The responses were interesting and honest.

What worked well	What did not work so well
Keeping voices gentle	Raising voices or shouting
Praising the child	Replaying past crimes
Talking with the child, not at them	Telling the child rudely what to do, ending up with non-compliance and escalating into an argument
Being interested in the child as an individual.	Not being interested in the child
Knowing something about the child's interests including family and friends	Not being clear, using innuendo and hints that were not understood
Getting down to the child's level for younger children	Assuming the young person understood
Asking the child or young person for their opinion	Trying to be 'one of them' with young people
Recognising an apology and not continuing to replay faults	Giving in
Listening to the child and verbally reflecting what they say, so they know you have listened	Not letting the child or young person finish what they are saying and talking over them
Recognising how the child is feeling	Walking away
Having eye contact	Demanding eye contact
	Sarcasm

Of course, you will have your own thoughts based on your experiences. This is not a definitive list, but aims to get you thinking about how you communicate with children and young people.

Consider the vocabulary you are using. Does the child understand what you mean? Think of this from the child's perspective. Have they got the vocabulary to explain their own feelings?

This may be particularly important if the child or young person has an underlying impairment such as autism or ADHD. Depending on the individual child, you may wish to consider using emotion cards to help the child describe their feelings.

Some children may need support to understand how their actions affect the feelings of others.

| Happy | Cross | Angry | Sad | Confused |

You may have noticed that 'eye contact' was mentioned in both columns of the table. Be aware of the individual characteristics of the child or young person. Some children find holding eye contact uncomfortable. Encourage eye contact, but do not force the child to look at you. This may lead to a negative cycle of influence.

It is important to know what type of communication is appropriate for an individual. We spoke earlier about unseen, underlying impairments. Some children and young people will take what you are saying very literally. Sarcasm and threats are not appropriate. We have already illustrated how Henry does not like eye contact, however...

> **Henry finds it difficult to hold eye contact. He will look elsewhere in the room. It feels like he is not listening or paying attention. However, on being asked what was said, he can repeat the instruction word for word.**
>
> **On occasion, Henry will look you directly in the eye and keep eye contact for a prolonged period. This tends to be uncomfortable for the other party. They will look away first.**
>
> **Although Henry may not be standing too close, he has invaded 'personal space' through visual contact.**

© The Play Doctors Ltd.

Communication needs to be individual. We are not all the same. Some people may require specific adaptations in the way communication is given and received. Think of a particularly stressful day when your mind is on something else. How often have you needed to ask someone to repeat something? Or you may have got the wrong end of the stick?

It will take some children longer to process the spoken word. Language can be very confusing. Keep your language simple and to the point. Give time for the child to process the information. If you are repeating an instruction, use the same words again. If you use different words, you are giving the child yet more information to process.

Some children will require the use of visual structure to support their understanding. This may be in the form of: visual symbols; signs; photos or objects of reference. For example, if you are saying 'hands down', hold your hands up and bring them down to the side of your body. This acts as a visual reinforcer to the child, indicating what you want them to do. Some settings use visual symbols via traffic light systems, to indicate if behaviour is, or is becoming, unacceptable.

Communication is a skill. Skills can be developed, honed and added to. The greater awareness you have of how you are communicating, the more effective you will be.

Conversations
Good conversations are meaningful, useful, involved and interesting. Something happens as a result of the conversation. Both parties feel they are being heard and understood. There is willingness on both sides to engage in a dialogue.

Having a dialogue engages both parties. You feel respected and involved. It is more likely that questions are asked and answers received. Information is clarified and understood. Don't assume the child understands. Ask for clarification.

If you are having a dialogue with a young person exhibiting challenging behaviour, be willing to listen, but be firm in the boundaries and rules that apply to the situation. It is essential to remain in control. Many young people have the skills to manipulate what is being said for their own gain, and misunderstand intentionally.

Bad conversation may go round in a circle with no conclusion, finish in an argument or feel unsatisfactory. One or both parties do not feel that they have been heard.

© The Play Doctors Ltd.

Think of a situation where you have been spoken to. How did it feel? Perhaps you felt de-empowered, unable to respond or make your view known. Do you ever 'speak to a child' without giving them a chance to enter into a dialogue?

Of course, sometimes a dialogue is not appropriate. If a situation is dangerous the child or young person needs to comply immediately. We need to teach children how to respond to this instruction.

A child on the autism spectrum who uses signs and symbols is unlikely to stop when the word is shouted. He may need additional visual support. This may involve holding up a card or stop sign.

Using dialogue to agree rules

Setting rules and boundaries is essential to generate a common understanding of what is acceptable behaviour. Some rules are set by adults; little or no consultation with children and young people takes place. If this is the case, then children may question why the rule exists. If they do not understand or see the value of the rules, they are unlikely to be obeyed.

Consider some of the laws of the land – have you ever questioned why a particular law exists? Take for instance, roadworks on a motorway. A forty mile an hour speed limit is still active for two miles after the roadworks have finished. This can be frustrating! We have no evidence to say why this rule is in place.

We can all think of other frustrating rules, limits and boundaries that do not seem to make sense. Think of this in the context of a child or young person. A rule stating 'no running' on the playground seems senseless. Why not run? What harm can it do? Children want to run while they are playing.

Some rules will only require you to obey them on occasions. Take the example above and consider: 'No running on the playground in icy weather'. This now gives a parameter to the rule. The rule has an explanation and makes sense to the child. In icy weather it is likely that you will slip and hurt yourself. Therefore you must not run.

Many rules are given in very negative language.

Don't .... No ....You must not ....

The child knows what they cannot do, but do they know what behaviour is acceptable? By developing and writing rules together with children and young people, they can own and self police the agreed boundaries.

When researching information for this book, we went to many settings. These included nurseries, after school clubs, children's centres, youth clubs and home environments. We observed how rules had been displayed and how well they were being obeyed.

Have a look at the examples. Consider the language. Do you feel the rules are positive or negative? Do you think that the children will understand the rules? Are the rules displayed in an attractive style? Do you think that children and young people have been party to writing these rules? Do you see the reasoning behind the rule?

Example 1:
Rules displayed in a nursery setting working with children aged 1-3 years.

- We play at nursery
- We walk and jump with our feet
- We line up at the door
- We smile with our teeth
- We eat food with our teeth
- We sit nicely at meal times
- We play with our friends
- We touch gently with our hands
- We share toys with our friends
- We keep our room tidy
- We always tell the truth
- We listen to each other

Obviously, when working with such young children, the rules need to be written by adults. However, it does not stop us discussing them with younger children and asking them if they think the rule is fair.

The staff at the nursery would refer to the rules and praise children for doing what the rules said.

The rules were displayed prominently in the nursery, surrounded by the children's work.

Example 2:
Rules displayed at an after school club for children aged 5-12 years.

| No running | No hitting | No kicking | No swearing | Don't enter | No muddy shoes in here |

No one is to enter the kitchen at any time!
No food to be eaten in the playroom

These rules were displayed on small coloured posters, pinned up on the walls. Some were on specific places such as the kitchen door. The room was not very welcoming.

There was no explanation given to these rules. The rules used very negative language. They must be obeyed. When asked, the children all knew the rules, but could not say why some of the rules existed.

Example 3:
Rules displayed at an after school club for children aged 5-14 years.

We have one rule only
RESPECT!

The one rule was displayed prominently in the hall. The setting had discussed rules with the children and young people. They had decided themselves that this single word reflected all the rules they needed.

All the children and young people had put their own handprint on the poster to indicate they agreed with the rule. When asked, the children were able to explain what this rule actually meant.

New members to the club were introduced to the rule by the other children. Explanations were given about what the rule meant, and new members were invited to add their handprint.

If a child broke the rule, other children in the setting would remind them what the rule meant. The setting had a good reputation for positive behaviour.

> We will have fun and enjoy ourselves, try out new things and make new friends
> We will always allow everyone to play that wants to do so; we will try to remember that everyone is important, including ourselves
> We will be kind to others, even if they are not our friends and we will make all children feel welcome and help them join in
> We will share our things in our play
> We will not ignore a child who is being bullied, and will try to stop it or go to a lunch time supervisor for help
> We will help other children if they need it
> We will tell the lunch time supervisor if they tell us not to do something. The lunch time supervisor will tell us why we cannot do it
> We will respect other people

Example 4:
Rules displayed in a school playground.

These were handwritten on to card and pinned to a small stand. The lunchtime supervisors brought the rules out during lunchtime, and put them in the corner of the play ground.

The first thing to consider is how many words are used. Do you think that children will stop and read all the information displayed?

The actual writing was in an adult's hand; not easy to read. There was little importance given to the rules. When asked, children were not able to tell us what the lunchtime rules were or where they were displayed. The rules are positive; however, they are too long-winded and complicated.

Example 5:
These rules were displayed on the fridge in a home with Mum, Dad and two boys aged 6 and 8 years. They were in the form of a poster that the boys had made themselves. These were placed around a picture of the family.

- We can go to bed late on Fridays!
- If we fight, we get to do 'time out'
- If Mum say's so, we have to obey
- If Mum says it's OK – go for it!
- If Dad gets involved there's no football

Obviously, these are personal rules, written and developed by the family. You may or may not agree with them. But this is how the boys interpreted them and wrote them up to display. The rules begin on a positive note and indicate an understanding of sanctions if they are not obeyed. Of course, it does not mean the rules are always kept!

Lastly, we have Example 6. These rules were displayed in a youth club for 13-18 year olds. The rules were displayed on a poster displayed in the main club room.

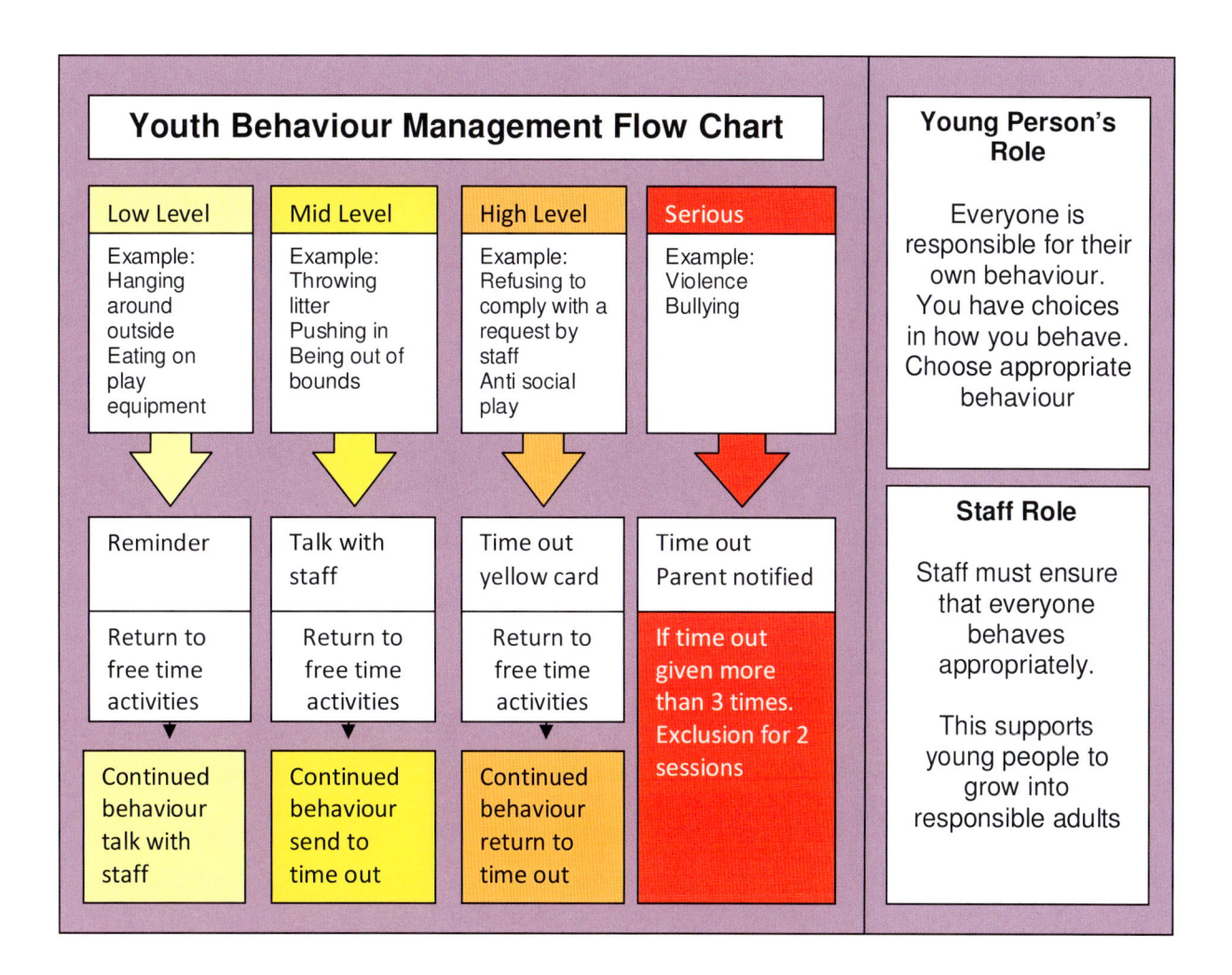

Youth Behaviour Management Flow Chart				Young Person's Role
Low Level	**Mid Level**	**High Level**	**Serious**	Everyone is responsible for their own behaviour. You have choices in how you behave. Choose appropriate behaviour
Example: Hanging around outside Eating on play equipment	Example: Throwing litter Pushing in Being out of bounds	Example: Refusing to comply with a request by staff Anti social play	Example: Violence Bullying	
↓	↓	↓	↓	**Staff Role**
Reminder	Talk with staff	Time out yellow card	Time out Parent notified	Staff must ensure that everyone behaves appropriately.
Return to free time activities	Return to free time activities	Return to free time activities	If time out given more than 3 times. Exclusion for 2 sessions	This supports young people to grow into responsible adults
Continued behaviour talk with staff	Continued behaviour send to time out	Continued behaviour return to time out		

It is likely that the club found this chart on the Internet and used it as their behavioural policy. It is certainly clear, indicating what will happen. However, it does not actually state what the rules are within the setting. When asked, young people said they did not give the poster any attention and did not really know what the rules of the club were.

Challenge: How would you start to establish rules within your setting either at work or at home? Remember the importance of discussing these with the children or young people. Make sure the rules are appropriate and support children to own them for themselves. Consider using visual symbols or visual clues to support understanding.

Cherry Trees After School Club decided that they needed to rewrite the rules to ensure that all children understood acceptable or non-acceptable behaviour. Instead of focusing solely on the child's behaviour, they asked the children to consider rules for everyone in the setting, including staff. Henry in particular loved this idea, making up rules for the play workers.

The club chatted to the children about the rules. Each child was given three Post-it notes. They could write or draw up to three rules each and put them on a graffiti board.

Once the children had written their rules, the play workers, along with the children, sorted them out. The children were only allowed a total of six rules. They voted on which rules were the most important. All staff and children discussed the rules. The children were invited to make a poster to display them. Each child's photograph was displayed around the edge of the poster. New children's photographs could be added.

Staff acknowledged that Henry and other children would benefit from visual clues to illustrate the rules. The children were able to draw, paint or cut out pictures to illustrate the poster.

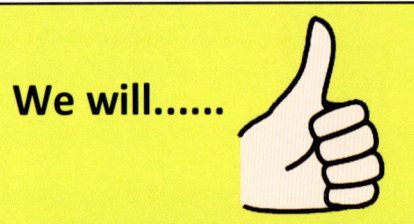

We will......

We will always be friendly
We will always share
We will speak nicely
We will listen to each other
We will look after our club
We will respect each other

The rules were:

Good practice: the rules
- are written in positive language
- are short and easy to understand
- are owned by the children
- are revisited on a regular basis
- ask for positive behaviour
- are understood by the children
- are understood by the staff

We each have our own way of determining rules and boundaries. We need to ensure that they are appropriate for the situation. Think back to the motorway speed limit when we did not necessarily understand the purpose of the rule. Remember that children and young people need to know why rules are in place and what will happen if they are broken.

Chapter Five: Consequences of behaviour

What is the consequence of the behaviour being exhibited? Earlier in the book we spoke about Henry behaving poorly so that he was taken out of a maths lesson on a regular basis. The poor behaviour was designed to result in a positive consequence. The consequence therefore encouraged the same behaviour to happen again and again to achieve the result the child has in mind.

It can be very hard for us to decide what the consequences of behaviour should be. Does the child know what the consequences will be, or is the adult offering empty threats that have no meaning? We each have an opportunity to influence behaviour based on the consequence!

> **Amy is going to the supermarket with her mum. She wants some chocolate. As soon as they get into the car, Amy starts asking her mum to buy her a chocolate bar. As soon as they get to the shop, Amy asks her mum again.**
>
> **Mum tells Amy that she needs to be a good girl until they get to the checkout.**
>
> **Two minutes later, Amy begins to play up. "I want Chocolate! I want chocolate!". She runs away from her mum down a different aisle. Her mum chases her and picks her up. At this point, Amy starts to scream and kick her legs. Mum puts Amy in the trolley. She is very conscious of the other customers and is embarrassed by her daughter's behaviour.**

Mum now has a choice to make regarding the consequence of Amy's behaviour. Her choices will be influenced by her own emotions. If she feels embarrassed in front of other shoppers, she may just want Amy to behave. She may do this by giving in, allowing Amy to have the chocolate there and then. Anything for a quiet life!

She may be cross with Amy for embarrassing her and decide to leave the shop altogether. Therefore, Amy does not get her chocolate.

She may tell Amy that it was her choice to behave in the way she did and the consequences mean no chocolate. Ignore her response and temper tantrum and ignore other customers' looks. Carry on shopping without purchasing the chocolate.

© The Play Doctors Ltd.

Perhaps Mum will take the consequences one step further: tell Amy her behaviour is unacceptable; refuse to buy chocolate and refuse to buy her favourite cereal as a punishment.

Each choice has its own consequence. Amy's future behaviour will be determined by what happens as a result of her current behaviour.

Consequence	How it affects future behaviour
Desirable – Amy gets her chocolate	Likely to be repeated to get another positive result
Not desirable – the shopping trip is terminated	Will probably not occur again in the same situation. Amy may still 'try it on' another time.
Nothing – the behaviour is ignored	There is no benefit to Amy in having the tantrum. The behaviour has not given her what she wants. This type of behaviour is unlikely to occur again
Unpleasant – the behaviour had a tangible consequence	The behaviour is unlikely to occur again and Amy will remember the consequence. She did not get her chocolate, neither did she get her favourite cereal

Go back to the initial story. Mum only set boundaries for Amy after she had asked for chocolate. Perhaps she could have offered Amy an incentive for good behaviour before they went shopping. She would then have understood the boundaries. "If you are good girl all the way round the shop until we reach the till, you can choose a bar of chocolate to eat in the car on the way home". The incentive is given; the rules are set. There is a positive consequence for good behaviour, in the form of a reward. Don't think of this as a bribe. Think of it as a reward for helping.

In this story, Amy is not involved in the shopping expedition, neither has she been given any responsibility. It is likely that she will be less bored and more engaged if Mum asked her to help write her a shopping list, help fetch items from shelves, asked for her opinion and offered choices. Think about how you can involve the child in activities and engage them in participation.

When we look at motivation we need to consider the individual child or young person. We have previously mentioned that some children do not respond well to verbal praise. Some children will be better motivated if offered something tangible that relates to their interests.

> **John is on the autism spectrum. He has a fascination with trains. If he was allowed, he would play with them for twelve hours a day. At school, he is asked to undertake particular tasks. If he has completed the task he is allowed to take down his train and play for five minutes. The time is marked through the use of a large sand egg timer. For John, this is more effective than providing social praise or a sticker.**

Negative consequences

We have written previously about positive consequences and how effective these can be in managing behaviour before it has happened. We now need to look at children and young people's understanding of what will happen if the behaviour they display is unacceptable.

Remember to ensure children are given a choice of behaviour. We do not always have to use negative consequences if the child makes a choice to change the behaviour they are exhibiting.

Always ensure the consequences are appropriate. Don't threaten a consequence without following it through or the child will not believe your threats in the future. Once a consequence has been applied, remember the issue has been dealt with and should be forgotten. The 'clean slate' syndrome should apply. Next time a negative consequence is necessary don't bring up past misdeeds.

Consequences may include:
- Doing something the child or young person does not like doing
- Loosing something that they enjoy

If the negative consequence is determined by the adult, the child may choose to blame the adult for the consequence. This may result in more negative behaviour. Some consequences can be negotiated and agreed as part of a behaviour plan or agreement.

We asked a group of 8- to 10-year-old children what they felt would be a fair consequence as a result of unacceptable behaviour. The children who contributed to this discussion all knew that there would be a negative consequence for unacceptable behaviour. They gave illustrations of the type of consequences they had experienced, and discussed whether they felt it fair or not.

© The Play Doctors Ltd.

Most children had experienced positive consequences, remembering trips out and treats. This was always linked to positive behaviour in their memory. When asked what happened when they helped out unexpectedly or did something beyond the expectation of their parents, most children agreed they were rewarded. Sometimes just with a thank you or a smile, which made them feel good about themselves.

The discussion with children was interesting. They all agreed that if a fair punishment or negative consequence was given it was okay. But they all agreed that it was not fair if they did not know what they had done wrong.

Examples were also given where punishment was not fair because the adult had not listened to the child and had given the child an unjust sanction. The children said sanctions had been given for something they did not feel was their fault. They said they were unable to get this message across.

The children said adults were not very good at listening. The adults wanted to be listened to, and told the children to be quiet, but would not listen back.

Two of the children knew how to 'get around' their mum by saying "Sorry" and "I love you". One child used the words "I love and respect you Mum. I agree with everything you've said". Apparently, this worked for him each time, with his mum responding: "I love you too", and then not following through on any punishment.

None of the children participating in this discussion had a say in what they felt were appropriate negative consequences. All said that their parents or guardian decided what would happen and for how long. Children were, however, given choices in relation to positive consequences, for example, what sweets would you like?

As mentioned previously, children may blame the adult for the sanction given, resulting in further negative behaviour.

The children's list of fair positive and negative consequences

Positive Consequence	Negative Consequence
Being bought sweets, a treat or surprise The children discussed the value of the reward and decided that the size of the reward needed to reflect what had been done to gain the reward. If rewards were given too often they lost their value and became expected.	**No sweets** The majority of the children were allowed sweets each day. They felt it fair if sweets were taken away for a good reason. Some children felt that sweets were taken away too easily. One child said: "Wasn't my mum a child before and didn't she ever do anything wrong!"
Staying up late The children discussed their normal bedtime routines and decided among themselves that a thirty-minute extension to bedtime was a reward. Some children had no defined bedtime so this reward would not be appropriate. Others 'banked' rewards for the weekend.	**Being sent to bed** The children discussed whether this was a punishment. They decided it was only a punishment if they wanted to be downstairs more than being in their bedroom. Most children had TVs and games in their rooms, so were able to play. One child said if he got sent to bed his dad took away his Game Boy.
Have a friend over The children agreed this was only a reward if it was unexpected or if there was a treat involved. Perhaps the friend could stay the night or they were allowed to order pizza.	**Take away mobile phone** The children decided this was the worst punishment. Even at 10 years old all the children had mobiles and used them to keep in contact with friends.
Watch a film Again, this was agreed a reward if it was not a normal family activity.	**Do washing up or empty dishwasher** The children didn't like it but thought it an acceptable punishment.
Earn a point towards a big treat This example was used mostly in a school or play setting.	**Points being taken away** The children felt this fair. They all knew that they could earn points back again.
Go out Again, this needed to be unexpected or out of the norm to be seen as a reward. Examples of trips out included: • Going to the skate park • Going swimming • Going to the swings on their own • Going to the forest and climb trees	**Vacuum carpets or sweep** As above, this links into doing jobs. Children felt it fair that they needed to 'pay back'. Jobs illustrated included: • Cleaning guinea pig hutch • Washing dog • Hanging out washing • Cleaning shoes
Do something with someone This type of reward was one of the favourites. Discussion showed that the children wanted to be given 'me time' and have someone do something with them. Examples given included: • Going cycling with Dad • Mum putting dye in my hair • Football with stepdad • Mum teaching me '*Chopsticks*' on the piano	**Sit on the stairs for time out** The children discussed this for some time. None of them liked having to have time out. One child was sent to his bedroom where he could play, so it didn't matter. Others had to stand in the hall, sit on the stairs, and one was sent out into the garden for five minutes until he calmed down.

© The Play Doctors Ltd.

Consider involving children in a discussion about positive and negative consequences. It can become part of the positive behaviour strategy in a setting or behaviour management plans for individual children. It will help children look at the ownership of behaviour.

We took the headings that were agreed by the group of children in the positive/negative consequence table and created a Consequence Spinner.

If the child is due a positive consequence they get to spin the dial and see what reward they will receive. The same applies for unacceptable behaviour, and this becomes part of the choice. "You can sit nicely and join in, or you can spin the spinner".

Each consequence is discussed and agreed. They are written out and made into a simple pie chart. The arrow is affixed using a simple split pin, allowing it to be spun freely.*

It is possible to still allow leeway. For instance, the spinner does not stipulate how long time out is, or how many times the young person needs to vacuum the carpet or wash the dog!

There may be times where this is not appropriate to use, and the adult needs to identify a sanction fit for the behaviour.

The positive consequence spinner can be used before an activity. "If you are helpful all the way round the supermarket then see what you will get by spinning the spinner."

Remember, this idea needs to be personalised by the individual child or group of children. The sanctions put into place need to have been previously agreed with them through negotiation and discussion.

Consider consequences in relation to the behaviour you are managing. What are the consequences for the children you are working or living with?

*note spinners are available from www.theplaydoctors.co.uk

Chapter Six: Encouraging positive behaviour

The face is the mirror of the mind and eyes without speaking confess the secrets of heart!

This was written by Saint Jerome (AD 374-419). It is very true, and we can learn through this by considering how we are using our faces and eyes to support positive behaviour.

This chapter is a toolbox of ideas. Not all ideas will work with all children. Experiment and be willing to think 'outside the box'. Use this chapter as a launch pad to develop your own ideas based on the knowledge you have of the child in your care.

Redirected behaviour If a child or young person is expressing emotion through behaviour such as anger, the behaviour may be destructive to themselves or others. By stopping the behaviour we may be storing difficulties up for a later date. The behaviour itself may stop, but if anger is not released it may only be a temporary solution. Sometimes, we all need to release our emotions, but in a safe manner.

You will need to use your own judgement. If the child or young person needs to release aggression, the following ideas may support redirected behaviour. If the child wants to kick and punch, consider similar movement activities where aggression is taken out on an object, not another person.

Jessica sometimes feels very angry. When this happens she will strike out at whoever is nearest. Staff at the after school club are able to tell when she is getting angry and aim to divert the emotions into a safe activity.

One play worker drew concentric circles on a white plastic tablecloth, creating a bullseye scoreboard. Jessica was given a large bucket of play dough. She was able to tear off lumps of dough and throw them safely at the scoreboard, which was spread on the floor (outside if possible and away from other children).

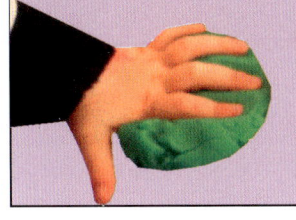

Once Jessica got her own emotions in check, she decided, of her own volition, to develop a game with the play worker, scoring each hit to see who won.

© The Play Doctors Ltd.

Consider the following ideas to redirect behaviour:

- Swing ball (remember Jessica's story).
- Tearing paper or leaves.
- Draw or scribble on a graffiti board, paper or chalk board.
- Rough and tumble play – children enjoy being wrapped in duvets, rugs or blankets. Try rolling children around using firm pressure. This technique can also be used to support calming. Be aware of sensitivities around touch. Also consider cultural boundaries.
- Structured and safe sports such as boxing or kick boxing.
- Physical activity including running circuits, high jumps, long jumps, skipping or swimming, among others.
- Provide an activity with an acceptable risk, concentrating focus such as rock wall climbing. Consider activities where the child's self-esteem and confidence will grow.
- Screaming into a cushion or bucket.
- Squeezing ice cubes hard and letting them melt.
- Making bread and kneading dough.
- Playing with stretchable putty.
- Soft ball play in a safe environment.
- Kicking piles of leaves, stamping in puddles.
- Trampolines.
- Ball ponds.
  - Water fights using water sprays, playing in a safe environment.
  - Blowing up balloons, bursting balloons and safe balloon fights.
  - Cleaning, sweeping, polishing.

What else can you think of?
We do not always have to impose sanctions. When dealing with anger or other challenging behaviour, provide the child with an opportunity to recognise when they need time out.

Depending on the individual, agree a signal that you will recognise to indicate that the child or young person wants 'out' for a short while. Some children will be happy to hold up a red card asking for a two-minute break. Others may give you a hand signal or other indication. Be aware that some children will want to manipulate this to their own advantage. Know your children, and ensure any quick breaks given are time limited and appropriate.

Warnings, choices and sanctions

Does the child or young person know their responsibilities? Before we look at potential sanctions we need to ensure the child knows what is and is not acceptable. Think back to the section on rules and boundaries.

Consider the child or young person. Get to know their interests, and work with them rather than against them. We have already explored the fact that many children respond better to visual structure rather than verbal.

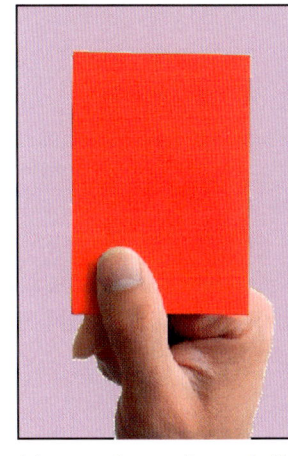

> **Henry responds well to visual stimuli. He enjoys football and understands the concept of being given a yellow or red card.**
>
> **His teacher uses this interest to let him know when his behaviour is not acceptable. A yellow card is given as a warning. At this point he will often remove himself from the situation. If he is given a red card he understands the consequences of his behaviour.**

Use what the child is interested in. Perhaps the child enjoys motor racing. If so, they may understand the concept of a pit stop for time out. An interest in trains may result in the use of a signal card – using train signals for stop and go. A child interested in numbers may respond better to numbered behaviour cards. Common systems include the use of traffic lights symbols or signs such as thumbs up/thumbs down.

If you are using a warning system, for example, the use of a yellow card, the child must understand their choices. If they do not understand what will happen they may not see any alternatives to their behaviour.

Often, children do not recognise how others may feel. Some may have a lack of empathy. Visual emotion symbols support children to empathise with how others are feeling.

hands   down

Try not to use negative language. Instead of saying: "Don't punch", start by giving a positive instruction to stop immediate behaviour, such as "Hands down" or "Feet on floor". Reinforce with body language, voice tone and, if appropriate, visual symbols.

Consider how you are giving choices. They may be linked to sanctions or negative consequences to behaviour. "If you sit nicely and carry on with the task, you can go out to play with the others at break", or "If you continue to kick the table then you will be staying in at playtime to clean under the tables with the dustpan and brush."

Other ideas include:

Withdrawal of something the child enjoys.
What does the child enjoy doing? It may be computers, television, football, sweets? There is a value in teaching the child there is a consequence to behaviour by withdrawing privileges. Make this 'real time' and 'meaningful'. Do not threaten a sanction and then not carry it out. Do not carry out a sanction too long after the event or it will have no meaning and will not necessarily be associated with the behaviour exhibited. "Right, you carried on that behaviour, so you will not get a chocolate bar when I go shopping next Wednesday".

Even though the chocolate is bought regularly on a Wednesday and it is something the child enjoys, the reason for the sanction may have been forgotten. If the sanction is carried out, anger may result. "It's not fair!" or more likely the sanction will have been forgotten and the behaviour remains unpunished.

Withdrawing something the child has earned.
Earning systems can be very powerful and used in different ways both as a positive and negative consequence. Have you ever worked really hard to save for something you want? Once the target is reached the sense of achievement is powerful. "I did that, I worked hard and I got that."

If something happens and the savings are taken for another use or lost, we have a sense of disappointment. If the reasons the savings are gone are down to our own behaviour, we may be disappointed in ourselves and have a desire to improve. We want to replace the lost savings as soon as possible to continue our aim towards the goal.

© The Play Doctors Ltd.

The principle is the same when managing behaviour. It is important to use earning potential to get the best from the children and young people we are working with. This can be done individually or in a group. If a group are working towards a final goal, anyone in the group who jeopardises the end result will feel the disapproval of the whole.

> **Jack's class are working towards an end of term achievement reward. If they work together or individually they are awarded points. The number of points gained can be exchanged for a range of class rewards from a class trip going white water rafting, a trip to the cinema, go-karting, or an afternoon off.**
>
> **Points can be awarded or taken away. Jack is aware that his classmates would disapprove if his behaviour meant that class points were taken away. For a short period while this system was in place, Jack's classroom behaviour improved. He did not gain the class any points, but neither did he lose any.**

It is possible to use this system as a sanction, providing any reward lost can be earned back. The children need to know this. Rewards should be awarded for agreed targets but also awarded for spontaneous positive behaviour such as helpfulness, support for others, kindness, etc.

If a reward system is being set in place for a particular child, remember to consider their own interests. A child interested in Thomas the Tank Engine may like a reward system based on the characters in the stories.

1	2	3	4	5	6	REWARD
						Buy a new Thomas the Tank Engine DVD
Because you tidied your room	Because you played nicely with your sister	Because you helped mummy with the shopping	Because you helped set the table for dinner	Because you vacuumed the lounge	Because you washed the dog	

© The Play Doctors Ltd.

Note in the example the reason for the reward has been given. This provides positive reinforcement for future behaviour. The character stickers are given to the child to place on the chart themselves.

This example uses a clock face or colour wheel, where the hand can be moved forward or backwards depending on a positive or negative consequence of behaviour. Once the hand has gone all the way round the clock to the star, a specific reward is given.

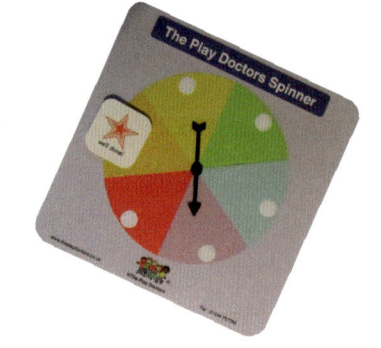

Other ideas include a marble run, where marbles are posted down a transparent tube. Once full, the reward is given. A negative consequence would mean a marble is removed, but could be re-earned.

What about collecting leaves on a behaviour tree? Leaves are given for good behaviour, taken away for poor behaviour. Once the tree has all its leaves, a reward is given.

Challenge: What other ways can you think of to give rewards?

When working with a child or young person to improve behaviour, consider your own language. Never dare a child to do something without knowing what the consequences will be. By saying "Don't you dare do that!" it may just encourage the child to do the behaviour all the more. If the child does not know what will happen as a consequence of their behaviour they may just be thinking "Well, why not?"

Time out and removal from a situation is an important technique. Be aware that this may be exactly what the child wants and that the behaviour may be designed to cause this. This may happen if the time out is more attractive than the activity they are being asked to do.

Consider the place you are using; don't use a place the child wishes to be. Their own bedroom may not be appropriate. Consider using a flexible space that can be moved to the child, particularly if the child is a danger to himself or others. Remember to safeguard yourself and do not put yourself in danger. Try sitting the child inside a hula hoop or on a carpet square; this provides a boundary that the child can recognise and understand.

Ensure the child knows the amount of time they are expected to stay there. If appropriate, use a sand timer to indicate the passage of time. Some children will respond better to a clock or alarm. If the child moves off then replace them firmly. Repeat the reason why they are there and tell them each time they move that the time goes back to the beginning again. The more they move off, the longer they will be asked to remain. This may take a while to work, but the child will soon learn that if they misbehave they will be expected to have time out.

Some children will eventually take themselves off for a time out, when they recognise their behaviour is unacceptable.

Don't delay in giving time out. Be consistent so the child knows what time out means and what to expect. It is important for you to decide on an appropriate length of time. Generally, one minute per year of age is acceptable.

A father was recently prosecuted for child abuse when he made his son stand outside for ninety minutes on a freezing night! This was not an appropriate form of time out.

Calming methods

Again, know your own child. Understand what they like to calm them. If they have a particular item that they use to calm down, take it out with you.

If you are working in a setting, consider the information you ask for in the registration forms. Ensure you know likes, dislikes, sensitivities, communication requirements and calming methods. Some children may calm down using unusual methods.

Kylie has autism. She sometimes gets very stressed when she does not know what is going to happen next. She has difficulty in thinking and planning ahead. When she gets distressed she starts to kick and scream.

Kylie will calm down if she is given leaves to tear and shred. She also enjoys smelling the leaves and after a few minutes will be her normal, cheerful self.

Have a think about the reason behind the behaviour, if known. If the child is upset, time out may not be appropriate but calming may be what is needed.

© The Play Doctors Ltd.

The following are tried and tested ideas for calming. However, be selective and aware of the individual child or young person.
- Hiding places such as dens, pop-up tents, under tables, quiet corners, under blankets and duvets. Try to ensure these places are low arousal. Don't use lots of bright colours or busy, noisy toys. Instead, consider calming colours such as lilac, pale blues and pale greens.
- Use of sensory play such as gentle lights, torches, soft music. Soft things to touch such as cushions and cuddly toys.
- Water play and bubble play. Also consider sensory experiences such as water mixed with cornflour, or a balloon partially filled with water that can be squeezed and manipulated.
- Walking and talking. Taking a child away from a situation and going for a walk around the setting, immediate or local area. Allow time to talk. Be interested in the child's hopes and dreams. Encourage them to think about what they are sensing: breeze, sunshine, rain.
- Younger children enjoy action songs that are repetitive, familiar and comforting. Older children often enjoy theme tunes from favourite shows.
- Consider gentle massage. Be aware of sensitivities around touch and cultural backgrounds. Consider using a soft wallpaper brush, brushed gently over a hand or arm. Soft, furry paint rollers are nice to touch.
- Bursting bubble wrap can be calming in several ways. Running your hand over bubble wrap gives a gentle massage or gently bursting one bubble after another using repetition to calm. Consider pouring a little baby oil on to a child's hand. The sensation changes as the surface of the bubble wrap becomes slippery.
- Gentle music and birdsong.
- Quiet story times and listening to stories or music through headphones.
- Try drawing in a shallow sand tray, running fingers gently through the sand.
- Experiment with fabric textures. Sheep's wool is soft and gentle to touch.

These are only a few ideas; you will have many of your own. Look around the room. What else could be used as a calming method?

Jack enjoys drawing. His grandmother bought him some glass chalks and he draws graffiti designs on his bedroom window. He finds this very calming.

Think ahead, to support the prevention of potential problems. Be proactive rather than reactive. When looking at children whose behaviour is poor when faced with sensory overload, consider:
- Some children who are noise sensitive may wish to wear ear protectors, earmuffs or headphones to cut out some of the stimulation.
- Those that are light sensitive may prefer to wear dark glasses.
- Some children may prefer to work independently if they are sensitive to personal space being invaded.

> **James attends a local youth group. He has mild learning difficulties and hates anything to do with writing. The youth group asked the children to write down their suggestions for future activities. James' response was immediate refusal and anger. He picked up others' suggestions and tore them up. His anger was based on embarrassment. His own writing skills were very poor. How could the setting have managed this differently?**

> **Henry finds it difficult to define his own space. When sharing a table he will grab things that do not belong to him and put his own things in other people's space. His teacher uses masking tape to clearly define his side of the table. The tape creates a 'Henry's frame', a localised personal space. This provides a tangible outline boundary. Henry finds it easier to keep to his own space when he can see the boundary clearly. If he accidently forgets, he is reminded to keep his work inside his Henry's frame.**

Other calming techniques to teach children and young people
If children can take a few seconds to think about their response to a situation they will have more control and be able to express their feelings appropriately. They will then be able to make their own decision about how to respond.

You may want to help remind the child to use a self-calming technique by using a 'key word' that is private and individual to them.

Jessica's teacher reminds her by saying: "Remember Malcolm". Jessica thought this was funny as the first four letters of 'Malcolm', are in the word 'calm'. On this reminder she learnt to use a self-administered calming technique she had been shown.

Suggestions include:
- Counting backwards from ten or twenty (this concentrates the mind).
- Deep breathing techniques (in through nose and out through mouth).
- Self-removal from a situation into a quiet place.
- Hugging a cuddly toy or blanket.
- Having a warm bath.
- Think of somewhere that is relaxing such as a beach or a garden. Discuss this with the child and find the child's 'anchor'; something or somewhere they feel happy. Do this while undertaking a physical activity such as:
    - Running a finger around a palm in a circular motion
    - Closing your eyes and turning your head from side to side slowly several times
    - Squeezing your thumb and index finger together slowly; releasing and repeat
    - Stretching all the fingers of one hand out and bringing them in slowly to create a fist. Release and repeat.
- Concentrate hard on one part of your body, for instance, your left hand. Talk to yourself and imagine that this part of your body is warm and heavy. Use your mind to focus entirely upon this and breathe slowly. Continue the technique, thinking of other body parts.
- Ask the child to scrunch up their face as hard as possible and, on a count of three, let it all out and relax. Follow this by scrunching up shoulders and relax; arms and hands and relax; and so on.
- Making a feelings book (writing down how you feel).
- Paint using calming colours such as lilac and pale blue.
- Use your hands to model clay, and concentrate on the sensation of this sensory activity.

> **Joe would come into the after school club in a very cross mood. It was difficult for the play workers to establish what the problem was and if they could help.**
>
> **The setting used two boxes, one with a lid and the other without. These were Joe's boxes. When he came to the play setting he was able to draw, write or make a model about what was bothering him. If it was something that someone could help him with he put it in the open box, and if it was something that was private he would put it in the closed box.**
>
> **His personal assistant at the after school club would ask him if he wanted to share anything from the open box. Through this method Joe disclosed that he was being bullied and needed help to know how to handle the bullies.**

Distraction and withdrawal

Distraction is about 'nipping it in the bud'; taking action before the behaviour becomes a major problem and redirecting attention elsewhere. Some distraction activities can also be used as calming methods.

Try asking the child to join you in doing something different. The example below shows that this particular distraction also acted as a calming method.

> **George is 7 years old. He has sensory overload and is unable to cope. When he wants 'out of the situation' he tends to run. At a holiday play scheme George was unable to run out of the front door and retaliated by biting and kicking his play worker. Another staff member was called to help, but George's temper was too much to control and he became a danger to himself and others. The Manager was called in to support and, on arrival, she stood back to make a quick observation.**
>
> **The two staff members were talking to George, trying to calm him down. They had offered him a symbol book to help him communicate. He was too stressed to use it, and threw it on the floor.**
>
> **The Manager recognised that George could not hear the words being used. He had got to the stage where he had sensory overload. The Manager stood in the corner and gently started to sing and do the movements to 'head, shoulders, knees and toes'. George was still angry, kicking the wall, but was listening. As the Manager continued, she did not look at George, so eye contact was not a threat. He began to repeat the movements with his hands. After a few minutes, he began to sing in a very cross voice: "Head, shoulders, knees, toes."**
>
> **It did not take long before George was singing with the Manager and sitting on her lap doing the actions alongside her. In this instance the song acted both as a distraction and a calming method.**

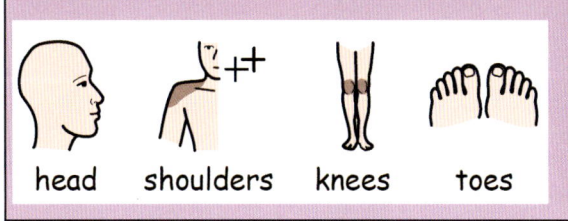

On occasion, it may be necessary to engineer social groups and withdraw certain children from situations that you know will lead to trouble. Be vigilant and step in when necessary. Separate children to avoid confrontation, and consider good role modelling.

For older young people who are behaving emotionally, try asking them a very random question. This will switch the part of the brain they are using and help to distract from an emotional response. For instance, an argumentative child or young person just about to 'kick off' could be asked: "If you had a baby rabbit, what would you call it?"

This is a totally random question that distracts the individual from their immediate action. It will not stop how the individual is feeling, but it will allow you to start up a conversation that distracts from the here and now. This in turn leads to a dialogue, and the young person may be in a better position to make sensible choices about what they do from that point.

Distraction activities may include:
- Offering the child a play alternative.
- Playing with bubbles, catching bubbles, making bubbles with a straw, painting with bubbles, printing with bubbles, making giant bubbles.
- Action songs, encouraging the child to join in.
- Using noises to gain attention such as clapping, ringing a bell, banging a cymbal. It is better to use external noises rather than your voice; your voice will just compete for space in a noisy room. Be aware that loud, unexpected noises can cause a sensory overload for some children.
- Hold up your hand and ask the child to count your fingers.
- Give the child a task such as taking a note to another staff member. This moves the child out of the problem area and can help to raise self-esteem and confidence when the other staff member thanks him for his help.
- Give the child a responsible task to help them feel good about themselves, for example, giving out something to the other children, putting something up on the noticeboard, sharpening your pencil.
- Sequencing activities, particularly useful for children who relate well to structure and order.
- Physical movement and games.
- Playing musical instruments.
- Using sensory play opportunities.
- Doing the unexpected – changing the routine, perhaps by having story time early.
- Use humour to tell a joke; get the children to laugh.

Consider what activities would really stretch the child. Something that is new or challenging. Aim for a distraction activity that will build self-confidence and self-esteem, reducing negative feelings. The well-known phrase 'Prevention is better than cure' means it is better to stop something bad happening than it is to deal with it after it has happened. Managing behaviour is no different. If we put preventative measures into place we will not be worrying about sanctions, consequences and punishments.

Of course, it is not that easy. But, by knowing our children and understanding some of the messages behind the behaviour we can think ahead and prevent potential challenges.

Distraction activities can be built into regular breaks. If you are aware that the concentration level of a particular child is low or time limited build in breaks to allow that child to have a little time out. This will prevent potential behaviour 'hot spots'.

> **Henry hates maths. After four minutes, he starts to fidget; after six minutes he is making noises and tapping; and after ten minutes he is getting angry.**
>
> **Henrys' teacher knows this and understands his specific requirements. She has developed a system so that Henry gets very short 'micro breaks' throughout the lesson. As Henry knows this, he is better able to cope knowing that he will be able to have a micro break.**
>
> **The kind of activities set in place include: getting up to a sharpen a pencil; walking around the classroom one circuit and then sitting back down; walking to the end of the corridor and back (so that other children do not get distracted); and fetching a drink of water from the water fountain.**
>
> **Henry knows that he cannot abuse the system and that he is being given a privilege. If he abuses it, it will be taken away. During maths, Henry's behaviour and concentration have improved. Even a micro break allows him to come back refreshed.**

When we become emotional we tend to raise the pitch of our voice and speak louder. Good practice dictates that we need to speak calmly to children and young people. However, on some occasions, by doing that the gap between the child's emotions and our own is far too wide. The child is too emotional to be bought down by a slow, calm voice.

A strategy to support this is known as 'Pace, Set and Match'. Be aware of how you use this; it is not appropriate to all situations. Consider the starting point of the child – loud, aggressive, high-pitched voice. Consider the starting point of the adult – quiet, calm, slow and low-pitched voice

The child may just feel angry at you for not recognising how he feels. Pace, Set and Match is a technique where the adult starts at the same point as the child. Using calming words, but in a loud, fast and high-pitched manner.

During the ensuing conversation the adult begins to tone down their response, lowering their tone, slowing down words and drawing the child down with them. They have paced the child, and are now setting a standard to be followed. The child will respond to the adult's voice, slowly calming down, and will begin to match the standard set.

The emotions of the child will not disappear. However, the adult has supported the child to calm down and talk in a more rational way.

Many children benefit from the use of warning systems to help identify how their behaviour is being seen by others. This can support prevention by letting the child know they must make a choice to improve behaviour before they face negative consequences.

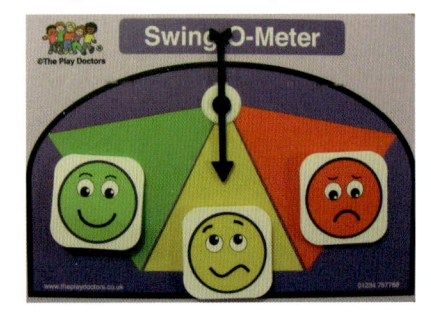

This can be done in many ways, including the use of visual symbols. We have spoken about using traffic lights or using something that is of interest to the child. Here, we take this a step further and offer a suggestion that is fun for the children to know if their noise level is getting too loud via a 'swingometer'. This can work well in a classroom or can be adapted for use at home or in a club.

Consider adapting the idea as a behaviour warning system.

Swing O Meter's have a variety of uses. It can help children to understand their own and other emotions, enable visual communication through symbols and for the child to indicate to the adult if they require any help by placing the arrow on a particular colour.

There are many ideas in this book; none of them is set in stone. They are there to provide you with ideas and to encourage your own thinking on ways of managing behaviour appropriate to the children you are working with.

© The Play Doctors Ltd.

Using music, movement and art

Music and movement can be very powerful in getting children to express their emotions. Start by working with something very simple such as a triangle or drum. Ask the children to make a noise that represents being happy. Work with the children to develop movements that represent being happy. Practise these for a while before moving on to other emotions such as sad, cross, upset, frustrated, angry, thoughtful, wanting to be on their own for a while, etc. Always finish a session with calming music.

Once the children have a repertoire of movements and music, try to expand the idea by adding other instruments and developing the movements. Experiment by introducing recorded music and asking how the children feel when listening to it. Take a note of music that the children like. You may wish to make a specific note of individual children's choices to use later. Look for music that makes the children feel calm and happy.

After the children are used to the idea they will be able to 'play you' how they feel. This can act as a safe way to display emotions for some children and become another redirected behaviour.

Consider making simple musical instruments with the children so that they 'own' their own noise making and can find their own instrument to express to you how they feel. It is preferable to listen to a loud drum being beaten, rather than having to stop one child kicking another.

It is well known that some behavioural management plans use art as a type of therapy to allow children to express themselves. You do not need to be an expert to encourage the use of art.

Ask the children what colours they find relaxing, friendly, sad, irritating, etc. Experiment with a list of words and match colours. Try blending colours together and creating a rainbow from angry to happy. Use this technique as a further redirection activity. Work with art to allow the child to express how they feel. After the child has had freedom to draw, paint or scribble, encourage them to change colours and use these to bring the child's emotional levels down by using calming colours such as lilac, pale blues and pale greens.

Colours are powerful in helping to reduce tempers. Think of your setting's quiet area. Does it have lots of bright primary colours, or does it have soft calming colours?

© The Play Doctors Ltd.

Strategies and ideas for specific behaviour

Biting
- Look for the signs. The more you know the child, the more you will recognise these. They may include clenched teeth, clenched hands and narrowed eyes.
- Remove the child from the situation immediately.
- Provide a replacement activity (for very young children this may be something else that they can bite on, for instance, a teething ring).
- For older children be very clear on rules; remember to use visual symbols to reinforce rules.
- Praise good behaviour.

teeth are for smiling

Tantrums
Avoid tantrums
- Look for the signs. The child will give you warning that they are getting cross. Try to divert their attention.
- Offer choices to the child – even young children want a level of control in what they do and how they do it.
- Set a good example – remember children copy behaviour. Raising your voice or displaying anger provides the child with permission to repeat the behaviour in the form of a tantrum. Give lots of praise when praise is due.
- Try to give very clear information and avoid words such as 'later', 'after lunch', 'in a minute'. The child will not know what to expect, and when.
- Keep trips as short as possible and try to let the child help (for instance, holding shopping, helping to take things off shelves, looking for items to purchase).
- Always remain calm.

Dealing with tantrums
- Ignore the behaviour, if not dangerous. This works better when the behaviour is attention seeking.
- Keep calm.
- Try not to respond in a negative manner; otherwise you will enter the negative cycle.
- Divert the child from the tantrum by offering an alternative activity.
- Recognise anger and look for replacement activities that will support the child.
- Use cuddles and security to reassure the child. If not appropriate, then consider wrapping the child in a coat or cardigan.

© The Play Doctors Ltd.

In-between years (7-13)
- Remember, young people are exploring their independence. Look for opportunities to provide choice and allow the child to be in control of their decisions.
- Listen reflectively; make sure the child knows that you understand how they feel.
- Praise behaviour that you wish to be repeated; teach by example.
- Don't give too many 'orders'.
- Never respond in kind; avoid arguments – use some of the techniques mentioned earlier in the book.
- Give fair warning and allow the child to make a considered decision about their behaviour (unless the behaviour is dangerous).

Not sharing
Practice co-operation games to help the child to learn negotiation and sharing. Suggested games include singing and action games (such as Simon Says). Use social stories to help the child understand how their actions affect others. Use positive words and ask the child to think of words to describe their own behaviour. Make a record of these words and display them. The child can be reminded of their good behaviour and remember being praised; this encourages repeated good behaviour.

Answering back
Ask yourself why? Does the child not respect you? Are you not listening to what they are saying? Are they copying others' behaviour? A powerful technique is to get someone to video a conversation. Watch the replay with the child and ask them how they would have wanted you to respond. Don't be afraid to ask why they answered you back. Listen carefully, and ask them how else they may have behaved. Have a conversation about what the word 'respect' means.

Being bossy
- Pay less attention to the child.
- Don't follow the child's orders; let them know that you are the boss.
- Remember, some children make the transition from being bossy to being a bully. Keep an informal eye on playtimes and ensure the child is not bullying others.
- Try to defuse power struggles by offering limited acceptable choices.
- Ensure all children are given the choices, and that the bossy child does not decide on behalf of others.
- Ensure your response has continuity, so that the child knows where they stand.
- Remember 'asking nicely gets…'

Chapter Seven:
Summary and further information

There are many books written about encouraging positive behaviour, and many websites offering support. Further recommended reading via websites has been listed on the next few pages. However, there are some very simple key messages to come out of the advice given.

Quick summary:
- Set goals with children about their behaviour.
- Explain what you want to change and why.
- Engage with the children to ensure those goals are realistic.
- Provide children with alternative behaviour.
- Ensure they agree the standards that have been set.
- Praise achievement and use positive consequences.
- Follow up on sanctions and negative consequences to unacceptable behaviour.
- Be consistent in your approach.

Try not to argue with other adults over how to discipline a child or young person or what sanctions to put into place. If children hear you arguing, then you are giving them permission to argue themselves. Discuss and agree ways to work together to ensure there is continuity over how you deal with the challenges you face.

There is never a 'one stop shop' in relation to managing behaviour. Try, try and try again seems to be the constant refrain. Don't get disheartened. Learn from experience, record what works well and remember what does not. Reflect on the experiences and consider 'why' as well as 'what'.

We are all different, and therefore each child will require a different response. You are not on your own; there are plenty of websites and books to help, including those looking at some very specific behaviour. Be prepared to do some research and to speak to others.

© The Play Doctors Ltd.

Take what you will from this book. Dip in and out of ideas. Reread sections to remind you, and share with colleagues.

Support other colleagues and family members. Remember, do not burden one person with all the responsibility for a particular child. Share out the duties of supporting positive behaviour, and ensure there is a continuity of approach.

Remember to communicate effectively with others in the child's life and to create a network approach to support the child. Bring consistency to your work in relation to behaviour management. Find out what tactics are being used at home, at school and at play.

Look for the good in everyone and praise what you find. Remember, behaviour diaries do not need to be negative; try to find something positive to write each day.

But most of all, enjoy the children you are with and give them childhood memories to be proud of.

Further information:

www.kidsbehavour.co.uk
This site has many ideas and strategies on behaviour management.

www.parentingcafe.co.uk
Support for parents when managing their children's behaviour.

http://raisingchildren.net.au
Support for those working with toddlers. This site is worth exploring for other support.

www.scope.org.uk
Behaviour management support for children with poor memory and communication.

www.practicalparent.org.uk
Support and advice on children's behaviour.

www.teachernet.gov.uk
Lots of support, including behaviour management for teenagers.

www.thecbf.org.uk The Challenging Behaviour Foundation supports behaviour management for children with severe learning disabilities.

About the author:
Wendy Usher has worked with children and young people for more than 30 years. She has managed various children's organisations and has been teaching adults for twenty years. Wendy started her business, The Play Doctors, in 2007 to concentrate on supporting inclusion. Wendy is married with two grown-up children and two grandchildren.

Other practical resource books include:

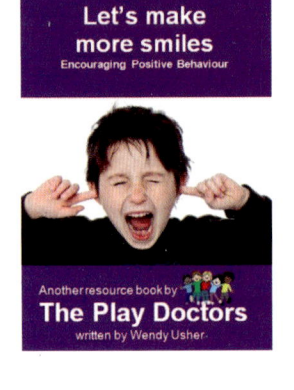

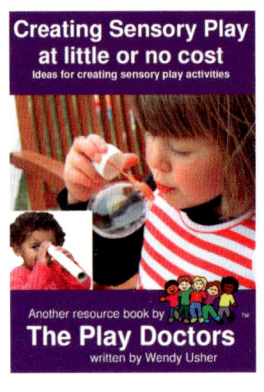

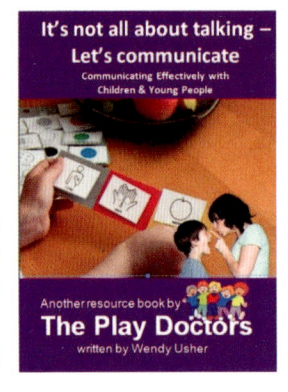

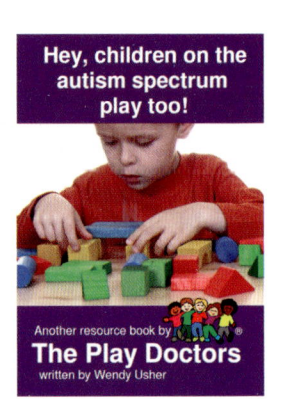

The Play Doctors also publish a range of children's books based on a group of animal friends. The characters have a range of impairments, and the stories identify how they adapt their games and adventures to ensure all the friends can participate. These children's stories have an accompanying adults' resource book full of ideas for creative play and activities.

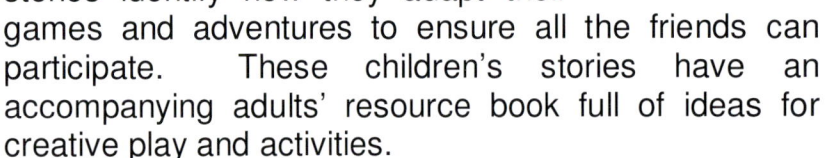

For further information about these and associated training courses please contact

The Play Doctors on:
01234 757768
email: info@theplaydoctors.co.uk
or www.theplaydoctors.co.uk

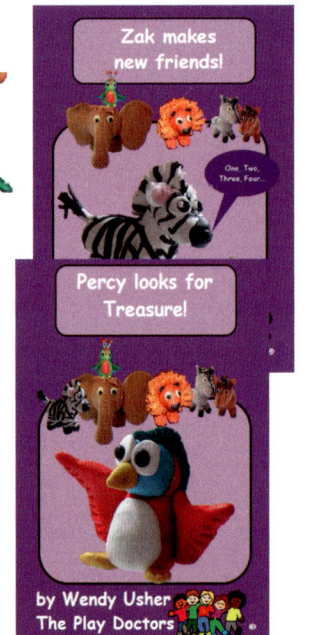

All rights reserved. No part of this publication may be reproduced, stored in retrieval system, or transmitted in any form or by any means electronic, mechanical, photocopying or recording.
Author Wendy Usher   © **The Play Doctors 2011**

The Play Doctors Publishing Company is a trading arm of The Play Doctors Ltd.

Reg Office: The Play Doctors, 13 Bourne End, Cranfield, Bedfordshire MK43 0AX